T0295522

Financing China's Belt and Road Initiative

Centering on the investment and financing infrastructure of China's Belt and Road Initiative (BRI), this book puts forth the basic principles and general objectives of constructing a new investment and financing system of this magnitude.

Beginning with a succinct analysis of the practical issues faced while developing the BRI's investment and financing system, the author puts forward several approaches to optimizing and reestablishing the system for the further advancement of investment and financing among and beyond the Belt and Road countries. Topics include credit rules, management and control systems, investment protection, dispute settlement and risk assessment while establishing a new mechanism that helps resolve debt defaults, checks for potential corruption and bribery, fosters new growth and enhances information transparency.

The book will be a practical reference for researchers interested in the Belt and Road Initiative and world investment and finance, as well as policymakers, financial institutions and enterprises relevant to the BRI.

XIAO Gang previously served as Chairman of the China Securities Regulatory Commission and Chairman of the Bank of China. He has engaged in monetary policymaking and financial supervision for years, and has a profound insight into China's macroeconomic and financial reform and development.

中国金融四十人论坛书系
CHINA FINANCE 40 FORUM BOOKS

China Finance 40 Forum (CF40) is a non-governmental, non-profit and independent think tank dedicated to policy research in the fields of macro economics and finance. CF40 operates as a "40×40 club" with about 40 influential experts around age 40.

The "China Finance 40 Forum Books" focuses on the macroeconomic and financial field with a special emphasis on financial policy studies to facilitate innovations in financial thinking and inspire breakthroughs, while building a high-end, authentic brand for think-tank books with top academic quality and policy value.

The "China Finance 40 Forum Books" has published more than 50 monographs and article collections in Chinese since 2009. Through its rigorous and cutting-edge research, this book series has a remarkable reputation in the industry and a broad influence overall.

Titles currently include:

Regulating China's Shadow Banks
Qingmin Yan and Jianhua Li

A Research on China's Economic Growth Potential
Chong-en Bai, Qiong Zhang

Financing China's Belt and Road Initiative
Investments and Infrastructure
XIAO Gang

For more information, please visit https://www.routledge.com/%20China-Finance-40-Forum-Books%20/book-series/CF40B

Financing China's Belt and Road Initiative

Investments and Infrastructure

XIAO Gang

Routledge
Taylor & Francis Group

LONDON AND NEW YORK

First published 2021
by Routledge
2 Park Square, Milton Park, Abingdon, Oxon OX14 4RN

and by Routledge
605 Third Avenue, New York, NY 10158

Routledge is an imprint of the Taylor & Francis Group, an informa business

British Library Cataloguing-in-Publication Data
A catalogue record for this book is available from the British Library

Library of Congress Cataloging-in-Publication Data
A catalog record has been requested for this book

ISBN: 978-1-032-02544-5 (hbk)
ISBN: 978-1-032-02747-0 (pbk)
ISBN: 978-1-003-18500-0 (ebk)

Typeset in Times New Roman
by Newgen Publishing UK

Contents

Figures

Tables

Acknowledgments

To make a deep and comprehensive research on the investment and financing system of the BRI, a research group which consists of senior researchers from policy-oriented financial institutions and commercial banks was established. I am pleased to acknowledge the group members for their great efforts and contributions. They are Wang Fujian, Li Ruimin, Zhao Yang, Xie Yongjia, Wang Jiaqiang and Liao Shuping.

Besides, I would like to express my gratitude to the interviewed financial institutions and enterprises participating in BRI, who also provided important reference information for research results. They are China Gezhouba Group International Engineering Co., Ltd, China Road & Bridge Corporation, China Three Gorges International Corporation, China Platinum Corporation, China North Industries Corporation, POWERCHINA RESOURCES LTD and TBEA, and a batch of financial institutions including the Export-Import Bank of China, Industrial and Commercial Bank of China, Silk Road Fund and China CITIC Bank (listed in no particular order).

XIAO Gang
February 2019

Introduction

Over the past five years, the Belt and Road Initiative has made orderly progress following the principles of wide consultation, joint contribution and shared benefits. In particular, investment and financing has yielded impressive results. The five years saw stable and smooth policy communications, frequent interactions among high-level officials of B&R countries and echoes and support from over 130 countries and international organizations. Connectivity of infrastructure and facilities has been quite effective, with maritime, land and air traffic developing in a coordinated manner; unimpeded trade has boosted close and frequent trade exchanges with countries involved in the Belt and Road Initiative, and an increasing trade volume; financial integration has played a greater part, with investment and financing services powerfully supporting related constructions; as B&R countries engage extensively in people-to-people and cultural exchanges, close people-to-people ties have become the important pillar of bilateral friendship between China and the other countries involved in the Belt and Road Initiative.

As per estimates of the World Bank and other institutions, B&R countries have a great funding demand for infrastructure and related investments but face shortage of funding supply, so more monetary resources need to be mobilized to support related constructions. B&R countries' complex environment involving politics and economy, ethnic and religious affairs, and social security may dampen the enthusiasm of investors; financial infrastructure varies greatly in these countries, investment and financing systems and mechanisms have weaknesses, and the soft connectivity of related rules and standards falls short. All these issues hinder investment and financing, and affect the progress of projects under the B&R Initiative (BRI).

Financial integration will make the economy more vibrant. It is an important goal of the BRI and also a key factor influencing the broad picture. Building a new investment and financing system which features openness and sharing can help address all kinds of existing issues in investment and financing, and thus ensure the initiative progresses as planned.

Investment and financing system generally refers to the organizational form of investing and financing activities, models and management methods of investment and financing. Specifically, it consists of investors and financing entities, investment and financing policies, sources of money for and models of investment and financing, supervision and regulation methods of investment and financing, and so on. Cross-border investment and financing systems also include investment protection, dispute settlement, debt bailout, risk assessment and early warning.

The new B&R investment and financing system will be built on the basis of in-depth research into existing investment and financing rules, financial infrastructure and financial intermediary services of countries involved in the BRI and the international community at large. It will be characterized by sharing of interests and risks, transparency of financing rules, high efficiency of operations, smoothness of multilateral communication and diversity of funding sources. Establishing a more open and sharing investment and financing system for the initiative can not only stimulate the activeness and enthusiasm of BRI countries but also attract financial resources beyond the BRI countries to join the initiative.

The B&R investment and financing work should explore how to improve the soft environment of investment and financing on the principles of pursuing innovation and integration, seeking common ground while respecting differences and adopting differentiated measures tailor-made to local conditions. It is important to strengthen the study of policies, standards and rules; perfect the bilateral and multilateral investment protection mechanisms; and step up the improvement of the soft environment, such as environmental and labor protection, for investment and financing. Besides, it is also crucial to put in place a debt default and bailout mechanism suited to the actual conditions of B&R countries, improve the business dispute arbitration mechanism, enhance coordination of financial supervisors and guarantee the functioning of the new investment and financing system.

What's needed first in building a new B&R investment and financing system is changing and improving China's existing investment and financing (export credit) rules, enshrining into them the inclusiveness and openness of Chinese capital, thus allowing Chinese financial institutions to lead and contribute in the building of the new system, displaying outcomes and benefits, and motivating other financial institutions to join the initiative through commercial interests in a bid to meet the demand of B&R nations to finance their economic development with collective efforts.

To solve the issues related to the B&R investment protection and dispute settlement mechanism, countries involved in the BRI should strengthen the talks on multilateral trade and investment protection agreements and sign, revise or renegotiate bilateral/multilateral investment protection agreements and all types of free trade agreements. On this basis, the nations should also develop a comprehensive protection framework for overseas investments, establish and improve an overseas investment insurance system and provide enterprises with all-around assistance, including safety and legal aid through consular protection, overseas security and judicial assistance, among other aspects.

Countries involved in the BRI should strengthen the B&R investment and financing risk assessment and early risk warning, analyze the issues in risk assessment and early risk warning in a timely manner, build a coordinated B&R investment and financing guarantee mechanism, establish a comprehensive risk assessment and early risk warning system, raise the holistic risk management awareness and capitalize fully on the advantages of policy-oriented financial institutions in risk identification, management and control.

The countries need to integrate themselves into the global debt resolution mechanism in innovative ways and form healthy debt coordination with Europe and North America. Besides, it is advisable to discover and learn from the essence and value of the debt resolution systems in force, heighten China's status and capacity in global debt resolution and develop a debt coordination mechanism that is embodied in inclusiveness and a disposition to learn from the East and the West. By bringing the dynamic role of original debt resolution mechanisms into full play, the debt issues of China and other countries involved in the BRI should be creatively incorporated into the global debt system, with benign interactions with organizations such as the International Monetary Fund ("IMF") and the Paris Club. Efforts should be made to standardize and strengthen the country-specific adaptation and debt sustainability investigations of investment and financing projects. Proceeding from the actual development state of countries involved in the BRI, the investment and financing projects must cater to the objective needs of economic development and the feasibility of national economy, and conform to the development level and debt sustainability.

B&R countries need to establish an anti-corruption and anti-commercial bribery liaison mechanism, a regular consultation mechanism and an information exchange apparatus, and enhance the transparency of the initiative's investment and financing information. Learning from the practice of multilateral financial institutions such as the World Bank, the countries should set up a blacklist system to ensure overseas operations comply with rules and regulations. In the meantime, financial institutions should co-develop and share the blacklist of entities involved in bribery and build a joint punishment mechanism.

Countries involved in the BRI need to publicize transparent information on the investment and financing under the BRI, fully disclose relevant information in the process of policy introduction and project implementation in a timely manner and make the initiative more attractive to various entities.

China needs to drive the internationalization of renminbi, improve the renminbi internationalization policy system, reduce the exchange costs of other countries involved in the BRI, ameliorate the building and supervision of financial markets and strengthen the ability to resist financial risks.

As an undertaking of the century, the BRI generates tangible benefits for relevant countries and acts as an important pillar in building a community with a shared future for mankind. To realize this lofty goal of mankind, a new investment and financing system must be established based on systematic endeavors. By studying and analyzing the practical issues faced by entities involved in investing and financing the BRI, I put forth the basic principles and general objectives of building the new investment and financing system for the initiative, and suggest recommendations for government departments, financial institutions and participating enterprises. I hope the project's research findings would contribute to the BRI.

1 Genesis and development of the Belt and Road investment and financing

During September and October 2013, General Secretary Xi Jinping proposed the strategic initiative of building the Silk Road Economic Belt and the 21st Century Maritime Silk Road (the "Belt and Road" or "B&R"). Working together toward building the Belt and Road is a strategic initiative proposed by China to protect the global trade system and the open economic system, encourage countries involved in the Belt and Road Initiative to strengthen cooperation and carry out concerted efforts to overcome difficulties and pursue common development, and build a community with a shared future for mankind. The initiative is epoch-making and of far-reaching strategic significance.

1.1. Overview of B&R investment and financing development

1.1.1. Value in B&R investment and financing

The Belt and Road Initiative (BRI) would be impossible without funding support. Investment and financing services are a key pillar and necessary condition for realizing connectivity of infrastructure and facilities and unimpeded trade. They are valuable in the following respects: first, supporting the initiative's funding demand; second, improving BRI countries' financial services; third, offering opportunities for the development of China's financial industry; and fourth, providing a platform for driving renminbi internationalization.

1.1.2. Achievements under the Belt and Road Initiative

To date, the BRI has received positive responses and support from more than 130 countries and international organizations. High-level government officials are visiting each other's countries more frequently, and the degree and scope of cooperation between countries continue to expand

and deepen. Positive results are seen in the connectivity of railways, highways, ports, energy and telecom facilities, as well as technical cooperation. As China's trade ties with other BRI countries become increasingly closer, the trading volume is growing year after year. From 2013 to 2018, China's trade in goods with other BRI countries surpassed US$5 trillion, and foreign direct investment exceeded US$70 billion, while the country paid US$2.2 billion taxes to host countries, and created 210,000 jobs. Investment and financing services have provided strong funding support for the initiative. Since its founding at the end of 2015, the Asian Infrastructure Investment Bank (AIIB) has increased its membership to 84, and launched 24 infrastructure investment projects involving total loans of US$4.2 billion in 12 member countries.

1.1.3. Chinese capital gives BRI a boost

First, Chinese government departments including the National Development and Reform Commission, the Ministry of Finance, the Ministry of Foreign Affairs, the Ministry of Commerce and the People's Bank of China have boosted the BRI by unveiling a full set of supportive policies.

Second, China's financial institutions have supported the initiative through participation in financial cooperation in diverse forms, and in doing so gathered rich experience. They participated in nearly 2,600 BRI projects, granted total credit of close to US$400 billion and loaned more than US$200 billion.

Third, the B&R investment and financing models and methods have become more innovative. Chinese enterprises tried various offshore financial resources such as related products and services of commercial and international financial institutions, such as HSBC, Standard Chartered Bank, Citibank and Multilateral Investment Guarantee Agency (MIGA), as well as using traditional export credit and trade finance.

1.2. Characteristics of B&R investment and financing

Although five years have passed, the B&R investment and financing system is still in its infancy. The 1.0 version has the following distinct characteristics.

1.2.1. Driven by policy finance

Policy and development financial institutions play an important part in China's economic cooperation with the rest of the world, and they help enterprises obtain credit support and hedge risks in the "going global" drive. Policy financial institutions are continuously reinforcing capacity-building. According to data for recent years, the Export-Import Bank of China (Eximbank), China Development Bank (CDB) and China Export & Credit Insurance Corporation (SINOSURE) have fully performed their policy and development finance functions, greatly supported foreign contracted projects and overseas investments of Chinese enterprises and played a crucial role in the B&R projects.

1.2.2. More extensive financial cooperation

The communication on financial policies involves wide-ranging content across many different levels, dealing with not only inter-governmental strategic financial cooperation in the macro sense but also business cooperation among financial institutions. This has made investment and financing services for the BRI possible.

So far, China has carried out useful endeavors in financial policy communication and coordination with other B&R countries, and the cooperation among financial institutions has achieved initial success. At the Belt and Road Forum for International Cooperation in 2017, SINOSURE signed cooperative agreements or MOUs with a number of peers, marking a substantial outcome of the investment and financing policy communication. CDB and Eximbank discussed potential cooperation with the European Bank for Reconstruction and Development (EBRD), and CDB also discussed joint lending with the French Development Agency (AFD). The China-CEE Countries Inter-bank Association, established in late 2017, is comprised of 14 banks and aims at providing development financing for projects in the two regions. It is set to become a fresh force in multilateral cooperation. The Belt and Road Inter-bank Regular Cooperation Mechanism of Commercial Banks has seen mutual referrals of projects exceeding US$2.5 billion among its 53 members.

1.2.3. Key support to infrastructure sector

Connectivity of infrastructure and facilities serves as an important foundation of the Belt and Road Initiative and enjoys priority in cooperation. It plays a pivotal role in supporting BRI countries' economic development and creating benefits for their people. It also provides significant support for realizing practical cooperation and mutual benefit for all. In the past five years, connectivity of infrastructure and facilities, typically construction of transportation hubs, petroleum pipelines and fiber-optic communication lines, has reaped fruitful results, successfully connecting Chinese capital and technologies with the infrastructure construction needs of relevant countries. Connectivity of infrastructure and facilities, visible in the emergence of a group of demonstration and milestone projects, has stood out as a fruitful leading area in the five-pronged approach (policy coordination, infrastructure and facility connectivity, unimpeded trade, financial integration and closer people-to-people ties).

1.2.4. Central and state-owned enterprises playing leading role

Central and state-owned enterprises have made irreplaceable contributions to the Belt and Road Initiative leveraging their strengths, mainly in terms of being strongly capable of carrying out a large number of influential projects which boasted big synergies and obvious driving effects.

Over the past five years, central and state-owned enterprises have launched many large infrastructure projects, fully displaying their robust professional capabilities. And they are good at countering risks because the market environment abroad is complicated, particularly the development of market economy in B&R countries is relatively underdeveloped, and some countries are politically unstable and highly risky. The Belt and Road Initiative is an updated version of the Chinese enterprises' "going-global" drive, with international cooperation not being limited to the efforts of single enterprises or single industries alone. Instead, central enterprises can bring their comprehensive power to the fullest and further enhance synergies and driving effects. In this way, a new model in which central enterprises lead a group of companies to go global together has come into being.

1.2.5. Industrial parks showing cluster effect

The ways of cooperation, management structures and development philosophies of foreign economic and trade cooperation zones mirror Chinese models and experiences, which can be copied by more developing countries involved in the BRI. Economic and trade cooperation zones abroad have already become an important carrier of the BRI.

Consistent with the B&R philosophy of "making joint efforts to a future enjoyed by all", industrial parks have injected fresh vitality into the Chinese economy and stimulated the further development of related service industries; they created more jobs and increased investments in host countries, galvanized the economic and industrial growth of host countries and raised social and economic benefits through expanding economic and trade contacts between China and other B&R countries, promoting their capacity cooperation, and drawing on one another's strengths. Through building cooperation zones, investors have attracted their domestic enterprises, and companies of host countries and other nations to set up plants there and form industrial clusters. This, on the one hand, increases employment and tax receipts of host countries and, on the other hand, helps them earn more foreign currency through export and improved technologies, thus spurring common development of bilateral economy.

1.3. Viewing debt growth in BRI countries rationally

1.3.1. Foreign debt of B&R countries

China upholds the principle of wide consultation, joint contribution and mutual respect in the Belt and Road Initiative. The country never forces any partner nation to accept the Chinese approach or encourage the partner nation to become debt-ridden but commits to promoting mutually beneficial and win-win outcomes that are shared by all. Moreover, the country follows international rules and commercial principles and engages in market-oriented project cooperation that regards enterprises as the main player.

As to whether the initiative has pushed the foreign debt of B&R countries higher, we can perform an objective analysis of the countries' foreign debt growth in the five years after the launch of the BRI.

The foreign debt of countries involved in the BRI is mainly made up of the direct borrowings or the medium- and long-term foreign debt guaranteed by the host countries' public sector. Due to the contingency in foreign debt changes over a single year, this report compares the annual growth of the medium- and long-term foreign debt of foreign countries' public sector in the five-year period before the BRI was launched (2009–2013) and that in the five-year history of the initiative (2014–2018) based on the IMF data. Our finding is that 37 of the 63 countries for which data are available have recorded a decline in annual foreign debt growth in the five years since the introduction of the BRI.

From 2014 to 2018, only 12 countries (Oman, Kuwait, Iran, Bulgaria, Nepal, Iraq, Moldova, Syria, Myanmar, Pakistan, the United Arab Emirates and Uzbekistan) reported an above 5% growth in foreign debt (Figure 1.1).

Judging from the statistics, the BRI does not push up the debt of countries involved in it. First, overall debt of most countries has not changed a lot; second, only a limited number of countries reported

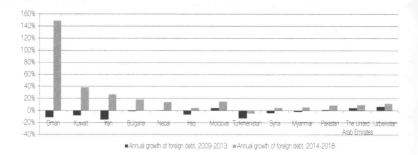

Figure 1.1 Twelve B&R countries with rapid foreign debt growth. Source:
         IMF Data.

growth in their public sector's medium- and long-term foreign debt;
third, in spite of certain growth in China's investment in some countries, the data refer to all of China's overseas investment, and the actual
data about sovereign borrowings or loans with sovereign guarantees are
smaller than such investment data; and fourth, excessively fast foreign
debt growth of individual countries has something to do with their specific development stage and national conditions.

1.3.2. Debt burden alleviated under innovative models of raising and using funds

Sovereign borrowings and sovereign guarantees are the primary reason
behind the debt burden increase of host countries. The debt issue can
be substantially eased when sovereign borrowings and sovereign guarantees weigh down. For example, changing the equity–debt ratio can
optimize the capital structure of projects, alleviate the debt burden of
host countries and scale up the investment in the B&R projects.

In recent years, due to the external economic and competitive
landscapes, Chinese enterprises have been innovating their overseas
business models and exploring different project financing models such
as public-private partnership (PPP) and build-operate-transfer (BOT).
They not only participate in the projects' planning, design and construction but also take part in the operation after completion of the
projects. In this way, enterprises can get immediate benefits from project
construction and, what's more, have access to future benefits, too, truly
expanding common interests and sharing responsibilities with host
countries. This integrated business model can also reduce host countries' debt pressure sharply.

In response to the debt issue of countries involved in the BRI, Chinese financial institutions have proceeded from the actual situation, strengthened the examination of the projects' self-liquidation during the approval process of credit funds, and provided projects with good economic benefits and in line with the host country's policies and easier access to loans. In addition, in view of the development state of different countries, Chinese financial institutions have adopted country-specific policies, and paid more attention to debt risks while supporting projects' funding needs.

2 Challenges faced by the Belt and Road investment and financing

Belt and Road investment and financing is hampered by an imbalance between supply and demand mainly due to three reasons. First, financing demand is massive in infrastructure construction; second, the funding is in short supply; and third, the external investment environment is complicated, and countries involved in the Belt and Road Initiative have big risk exposures on the whole. These three reasons are jointly responsible for causing a big funding shortfall in the BRI.

2.1. Huge funding demand

While funding for the initiative is struggling to meet the massive demand, it is hard to fulfill the needs of B&R countries and cross-border investment projects due to shortage of funding sources, lack of diversity in financing models and hampered financing channels (Table 2.1). Currently, sovereign loans provided by China are the main funding source of the Belt and Road Initiative (BRI).

2.1.1. Estimates of Chinese and foreign research institutes on financing needs of infrastructure construction

Based on the economic development level of BRI countries, the Institute of World Economics and Politics (IWEP) of the Chinese Academy of Social Sciences calculated the transport infrastructure investment requirements of the initiative, and estimated the needs at US$2.9 trillion from 2016 to 2030.

The Development Research Center of the State Council estimated the scale of desired investment based on the share of total in infrastructure along the Belt and Road at US$10.6 trillion in aggregate.

According to a report of the Asian Development Bank (ADB) in 2017, Asia and the Pacific would need to invest more than US$22.6

Table 2.1 Estimated infrastructure investment needs (unit: US$ billion)

Sector	Baseline Estimates			Climate-adjusted Estimates		
	Investment Needs	Annual Average	Share of Total (%)	Investment Needs	Annual Average	Share of Total (%)
Power	11,689	779	51.8	14,731	982	6.76
Transport	7,796	520	34.6	8,353	557	6.56
Telecommunications	2,279	152	10.1	2,279	152	5.12
Water and Sanitation	787	52	3.5	802	53	3.31
Total	**22,551**	**1,503**	**100**	**26,166**	**1,744**	**1.02**

Source: ADB estimates

trillion from 2016 to 2030, or US$1.5 trillion per year, if the region is to maintain its growth momentum[1] (see Table 2.1).

The World Bank estimated that the developing world's infrastructure investment requirements would reach around US$864 billion by 2030, including about US$649.9 billion from countries involved in the Belt and Road Initiative, accounting for the absolute majority. But the World Bank only took each country's infrastructure needs into consideration and did not take account of the cross-border infrastructure requirements.[2]

2.1.2. The project group's estimates on financing needs of infrastructure construction

Our estimates of B&R countries' infrastructure investment and financing needs are mainly based on the percentage of a country's infrastructure investment in a specific development stage in its GDP. The Project Group has made the estimates by following these basic steps: (1) estimating the GDP aggregate of B&R countries in the next five years; (2) determining the percentage of infrastructure investment in GDP in the next five years, and on this basis calculating each year's infrastructure investment scale; and (3) adding these figures together and getting the total investment needs of countries involved in the BRI for infrastructure construction.

The IMF's GDP estimates are taken as B&R countries' GDP figures during the 2018–2022 period. Figure 2.1 shows the estimated GDP aggregate of each region from 2013 to 2022. In the next five years, South Asia and Southeast Asia will see a robust growth in GDP aggregate, outstripping West Asia and North Africa to become the region with the largest GDP aggregate among countries involved in the BRI.

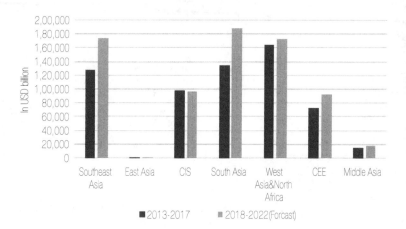

Figure 2.1 GDP of B&R countries (unit: US$100 million). Source: IMF WEO database.

Based on the estimates of the World Bank and the infrastructure development practices of B&R countries, the Project Group has devised three scenarios with respect to the percentage of the countries' infrastructure investment in their GDP during 2018–2022, i.e. high percentage, medium percentage and low percentage, with the average percentage standing at 8%, 7% and 6%, respectively.

We get the infrastructure investment amount by multiplying each country's economic aggregate with the percentage of infrastructure investment in GDP and then calculating the sum of products (see Table 2.2). That is, accumulative infrastructure investments in countries involved in the BRI will come in at US$9–12 trillion during the 2018–2022 period, and the annual investment will be US$1.8–2.4 trillion.

Accumulative infrastructure investments in B&R countries (excluding China) will reach US$4.5–5.9 trillion during 2018–2022, and the annual investment will amount to US$0.9–1.2 trillion (see Figure 2.2).

Global research institutes have also calculated future infrastructure investment needs. See Table 2.3 for summary results. Although their calculations vary sharply in scope and result, worldwide infrastructure project investment requirements are massive, even taking the lower band of the calculations. Moreover, it is not just the infrastructure sector that is hungry for capital in the B&R Initiative. Many other fields are also looking for money, such as government-led development financing and commercial investment projects initiated by private sector participants.

Table 2.2 Estimated infrastructure investment needs of B&R countries under different scenarios (in US$ billion)

Region	Low Percentage		Medium Percentage		High Percentage	
	Five-years' Aggregate	Five-year Average	Five-years' Aggregate	Five-year Average	Five-years' Aggregate	Five-year Average
Southeast Asia	1046.2	209.2	1220.5	244.1	1394.9	279.0
East Asia	4.0	0.8	4.7	0.9	5.4	1.1
CIS	581.7	116.3	678.7	135.7	775.6	155.1
South Asia	1125.9	225.2	1313.5	262.7	1501.1	300.2
West Asia and North Africa	1036.1	207.2	1208.8	241.8	1381.5	276.3
Central and Eastern Europe	552.9	110.6	645.0	129.0	737.1	147.4
Central Asia	106.1	21.2	123.8	24.8	141.5	28.3
China	4693.4	938.7	5475.6	1095.1	6257.8	1251.6
Total	9146.3	1829.3	10670.6	2134.1	12195.0	2439.0

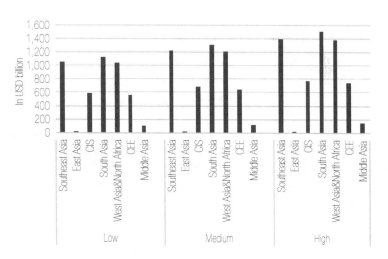

Figure 2.2 Estimated total infrastructure investment needs in B&R countries (excluding China).

Table 2.3 Estimated infrastructure financing needs of the Belt and Road Initiative

Source	Estimated Needs (US$1 trillion)	Coverage
World Bank (2013)	4.1	Developing nations
Asian Development Bank (2017)	22.6	Asia-Pacific nations
IWEP (2017)	2.9	Transport industry of nations involved in the BRI
Project Group of the Development Research Center of the State Council (2017)	10.6	Nations involved in the BRI (excluding China)
Final estimate of the report	9–12	Nations involved in the BRI

2.2. Insufficient funding supply

Funding for the initiative is struggling to meet the massive demand. It is hard to fulfill the needs of B&R countries and cross-border investment projects due to shortage of funding sources, lack of diversity in financing models and hampered financing channels. Currently, sovereign loans provided by China are the main funding source of the BRI.

2.2.1. Shortage of funding sources

2.2.1.1. Heavy reliance on Chinese capital

From the start of the initiative, China has been the main funder of B&R infrastructure construction. Among policy-based financial institutions, as of the end of July 2017, CDB lent US$170 billion to 64 countries involved in the BRIcumulatively, and the loan balance was US$110 billion; Eximbank signed over 1,200 contracts on projects in BRI countries, involving more than 800 billion renminbi. As for commercial financial institutions, as of the end of September 2017, Bank of China followed up about 480 significant foreign projects along the Belt and Road, and invested more than US$460 billion.

On the other hand, international financial institutions offered limited loans and grants. In FY2016, the International Bank for Reconstruction and Development (IBRD) and the International Development Association (IDA), both of which are World Bank institutions, only provided loans of US$45.9 billion, while ADB offered loans and grants of US$17.47 billion.

2.2.1.2. Limited capital from ODA

Official Development Assistance (ODA) funds, typically represented by multilateral development banks, have played an important part in Asia's infrastructure sector by not only offering capital, knowledge and technological experience but also coordinating all participants of recipient countries in a relatively effective way. But multilateral development banks mostly focus on local infrastructure projects in order to promote regional integration, and they seldom collaborate with each other. This leads to redundant projects or a crowding out effect, which increases the construction and coordination costs of recipient nations and weakens the connectivity.

2.2.1.3. Indifferent private capital

Private capital is indifferent to infrastructure projects because of the mismatch between risk and return. The participation of private capital and its effects are subject to a number of factors, such as economic cycle, government rules and supervisory capacity. Not all projects can attract private capital and bring good economic benefits. In some countries involved in the BRI, the political situation is unstable, government policies change frequently and the investment and market environment is not favorable. Even when private investors are willing to contribute to these countries' infrastructure construction, the countries' low ability to repay debt means they will struggle to repay principal and interest. Presently, only 0.2% of the infrastructure investment in Asian countries is by the private sector. The infrastructure investment in these nations, meanwhile, takes up nearly 7% of GDP.

2.2.2. Lack of diversity in financing models

2.2.2.1. Dominance of bank loans

Projects in the BRI have diverse financing needs. Currently, bank loans are the largest funding source of the infrastructure sector, while equity financing remains inadequate; in particular, the private sector does not have much interest in investing in infrastructure. A multi-tiered investment and financing system to make financing arrangements such as loans, equity financing, bond financing and ODA for the BRI does not exist. Although China has created some medium- and long-term funds (e.g., Silk Road Fund, China-Africa Development Fund and related industrial, regional and national funds), the quantity and role of equity investment are still very limited as far as the scale and actual operation of the funds are concerned.

2.2.2.2. Need to expand project financing models

It is clear that many countries involved in the BRI are poor at infrastructure construction due to underdeveloped technology and inability to manage and operate the projects. Project financing, particularly the PPP model, allows public and private capital to establish firm partnerships as a market-oriented and socialized innovative method of supplying public products and services. From this perspective, supporting the BRI countries' infrastructure construction via the project financing model has vast potential.

2.2.2.3. Slow development of bond financing

Bond financing remains a weak link in investment and financing for the BRI. Asian countries have made facilitation of development of Asian bond markets a priority of regional financial cooperation. The issuing of long-term bonds by AIIB will provide experience for the development of local bond markets. The B&R countries have reached a consensus on driving the development of local currency bond markets and increasing the sources of medium- and long-term capital.

2.2.3. Hampered financing channels

2.2.3.1. Lack of coordination between commercial and policy-based financial institutions

The line between commercial and political projects is unclear in the BRI. Commercial and policy-based financial institutions fail to communicate information smoothly or coordinate sufficiently. As a result, money swarms into some projects, but others do not have enough funding. Owing to the differences in business performance assessment of policy-based and commercial financial institutions, their business strategies vary, too. Consequently, some projects lack a holistic plan on which institution to tap first and how. Disjointed coordination between institutions will hinder the supply of funds for the BRI.

*2.2.3.2. Limited role of Chinese financial institutions in
stimulating the development in other countries and regions*

Chinese financial institutions are witnessing a quick growth of international business, but they need to further improve their capacity and
service to take on global competitors. The actual attention paid by the
headquarters of Chinese financial institutions to overseas expansion is
still less than what they pay to domestic business, and the resources they
allocate to international operations are not enough. Moreover, because
Chinese banks still place priority on traditional deposits, loans and
international settlement business abroad, they lack the product and service innovations suited for foreign markets, and find it difficult to integrate into local financial development environments.

In regard to the external environment, some economies are
suspiciousabout the entry of Chinese financial institutions, believing
that China's financial supervision needs to be enhanced and the
country's financial exposures are high. So they review Chinese financial
institutions' license filings more strictly, or even impose access barriers
on the grounds of forestalling financial risks.

2.3. BRI countries face high overall risk exposures

Countries involved in the BRI are generally exposed to high risks,
another key factor influencing the imbalance between fund supply and
demand. Political risk, including poor political stability, government
default, FX control, ethnic/religious conflict and geopolitical risk, is the
primary concern about overseas investment.

2.3.1. Geopolitical risk high and interest relationships complicated

Some countries involved in the BRI have frequent political conflicts;
some have been trapped in political turmoil, ethnic conflicts and
terrorism for a long time; and territorial disputes between certain
countries are quite fierce. The places the BRI crosses are directly
connected to Eurasia, so the geographical location is special. Some
countries and regions involved in the BRI are members of different
cooperative organizations sponsored and led by different superpowers
at the same time, and are of strategic importance to the geopolitical
game. This has a profound influence on related investment and financing activities.

2.3.2. Terrorism remains a threat

Terrorism in BRI countries is a major issue. Terrorist attacks and counter-terror measures frequently hit the arc-shaped zone spanning West Asia, South Asia and Central Asia. "East Turkistan" terrorist forces have long settled in Central Asia, West Asia and South Asia, and they plan and carry out terrorist activities from time to time. In recent years, the rise of new terrorist organizations represented by ISIS has posed greater threat to regional security along the Belt and Road.

2.3.3. Fiscal and taxation risks high and economic policies unstable

Most countries involved in the BRI are emerging economies, and they are vulnerable to external economic fluctuations. Especially when an economic crisis breaks out, these countries find it impossible to focus on their own issues. Therefore, they have to change their economic, fiscal and tax policies, leading to policy instability; furthermore, the political situation of some countries is unstable, and government changes result in poor continuity of economic policies; coupled with different national interests and economic development goals, different nations have different economic, fiscal and tax policies. Thus, countries and regions involved in the BRI find it hard to become interconnected, which, in turn, restricts regional capital flows.

2.3.4. Debt default risk and debt repayment pressure high

Some countries involved in the BRI have debt sustainability risks. In others, for political needs around ruling party changes and democratic elections, the administration is eager to publicize achievements to showcase their image. To this end, the government may disregard actual capabilities and propose infrastructure projects and programs for improving people's well-being without carrying out proper feasibility studies. Some nations do not have a domestic driving force for economic growth and count on other countries to provide support and momentum. They even compare how much support they have obtained from other countries.

Some Chinese state-owned enterprises tantalize borrowing countries in order to obtain projects, with a few even reducing prices to win bids. Financial institutions do not have uniform country risk ceilings and information is fragmented. Relevant government departments are not able to make overall plans, and some of them even invest for the short-term only. Therefore, unrealistic and non-standard project operations may increase debt default risks.

2.3.5. Metrics

Solvency indicates a country's debt risk exposures. There are three key metrics to measure solvency: debt service-to-export revenue ratio, debt-to-GDP ratio, and debt-to-export revenue ratio. Figure 2.3 presents the three indicators of some countries involved in the BRI in 2016. The three metrics of some countries exceeded the international warning levels, reflecting that their debt level was too high and debt pressure too big.

2.3.6. Cultural and legal risks are high and business environment is not ideal

A defective legal system will hinder investment and financing. Countries and regions involved in the BRI have different social systems and laws.

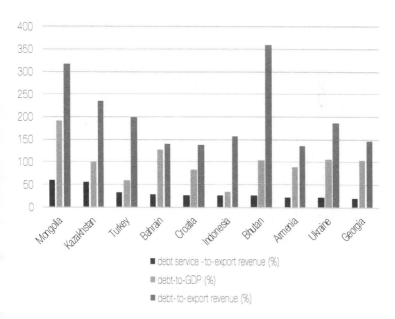

Figure 2.3 Three debt indicators of some countries involved in the Belt and Road Initiative in 2018. Source: EIU CountryData.

Chinese enterprises participating in their infrastructure construction and investment may face legal issues concerning environmental protection, labor, intellectual property rights, investment management and taxation, among others.

The business environment is another key factor influencing investment and financing. Most BRI countries encourage and support opening of new enterprises but do not have a proper legal mechanism to address poor operation, bankruptcy and reorganization of companies.

2.4. Soft environment barriers, a hurdle to B&R investment and financing

Apart from factors such as large funding demand for investment and financing of infrastructure construction, insufficient funding supply and high levels of risk in BRI countries, soft environment barriers such as inadequate support from existing credit policies, investment protection and dispute settlement, risk assessment and early warning, debt default and bailout, and non-transparency of investment and financing information restrict the smooth operation of the Belt and Road investment and financing.

First, the rules of Chinese financial institutions on financing terms, interest rates, China's content and approval cannot meet the huge capital needs of the BRI.

Second, bilateral, multilateral, and judicial procedures of countries involved in the BRI have such weaknesses as insufficient investment protection and inadequate dispute settlement mechanisms.

Third, in the face of more complex and diverse types of risks along the Belt and Road, existing risk assessment concepts, assessment structures and assessment tools need to be improved.

Fourth, the debt default and bailout mechanism cannot meet the objective needs of the BRI.

Fifth, some countries involved in the BRI do not have a complete set of laws and regulations, and their governments are inefficient and corrupt, which increases risks in investing and financing activities and project construction.

Sixth, lack of information transparency hurts the BRI's attractiveness to various resources and subsequent development to a certain extent.

Seventh, slow progress of renminbi internationalization means it is unable to play a due role in reducing the circulation costs and enhancing the ability to resist financial risks in the BRI.

In addition, insufficient innovation in investment and financing tools; the host countries' environmental, labor, and tax policy constraints; deficiencies in the host countries' financial services and financial supervision; lack of financial intermediaries related to investing and financing activities; and obstacles to the connectivity with industrial technology standards also affect the Belt and Road investment and financing.

Notes

1 Asian Development Bank (ADB),*Meeting Asia's Infrastructure Needs,* 2017. http://dx.doi.org/10.22617/FLS168388-2.
2 Fay, Marianne, Martimort, David, Straub, Stephane,*Funding and Financing Infrastructure: The Joint Use of Public and Private Finance.* Policy Research Working Paper; No. 8496. Washington, DC: World Bank, 2018. https:// openknowledge.worldbank.org/handle/10986/29949 License: CC BY 3.0 IGO.

3 An approach for solving the Belt and Road investment and financing issues

As the Belt and Road Initiative marches ahead and China proposes to co-build a "community with a shared future for mankind", China, the second-largest economy in the world, must seek a new approach to shoulder its responsibilities and cope with challenges.

3.1. The existing approach requires an overhaul

China's successful experience and existing Western rules cannot remove the barriers to the Belt and Road investment and financing in current situation. The existing approach needs an overhaul.

3.1.1. A Chinese approach alone impossible

First, China has not yet developed a systematic approach. A whole suite of investment and financing operation mechanisms which have been effective in China over the past 40 years of reform and opening up are not generally applicable to all the other countries involved in the Belt and Road Initiative. In practice, China has to consider projects case by case.

Second, existing rules in China are low in standard, unstable and not transparent and detailed enough. Rules readily acceptable to the international community should be stable, transparent, rigorous, operable and verifiable. Chinese rules and standards need to be aligned with these characteristics. And a process is needed for such rules and standards to be universally accepted by the international community.

Third, for different concerns, some countries have doubts about the BRI, and cannot accept the Chinese approach completely. This makes the launch of many investment and financing projects impossible. Some countries wish to get more money, technologies and aid from China, on the one hand, but are fearful of increased reliance on China, on the other hand.

3.1.2. Reliance on the West's international rules impractical

Objectively speaking, it took developed countries in Europe and North America or international organizations a quite long process to gradually improve their investment and financing rules and standards. The logics and ideas behind this reflect the general law governing economic development of advanced nations. However, direct copying of these rules and standards by countries involved in the BRI will not work because it does not suit the less-developed world where human resources are scarce. For example, foreign policies and standards on SOEs, environmental protection, labor and debt repayment, and so on, are more rigorous and do not fit the national conditions of countries involved in the BRI; and beneficiaries often have to carry out extensive policy adjustment plans under the funding support of IMF in order to get debt solutions from the Paris Club and the like. Hence, countries involved in the BRI cannot simply copy international rules.

3.1.3. Leaving the issues hanging in the air also unworkable

Regarding which kind of rules or standards to adopt, many countries, including China, do not use international rules or cannot develop better or externally recognized rules in a short time. They leave the issues hanging in the air, and do not or are unwilling to change their own rules.

As the proposer of the BRI, China urgently needs to integrate into the international community more quickly and reach consensus with them on some key rules and standards in order to realize wide consultation, joint contribution and shared benefits with the rest of the world. In terms of international governance, it is impractical and impossible for China not to be involved, make a statement or take a stand. In this context, China should either adapt to existing rules or improve the prevailing rules. Skirting around or delaying solving issues will not help anyone.

3.2. Basic principles for solving the B&R investment and financing issues

How to lift these investment and financing barriers and explore the new solutions to the Belt and Road investment and financing issues has become a common concern of China and the other countries involved, as well as advanced nations. We hereby put forth four principles for strengthening soft connectivity and jointly contributing to the improvement of the soft environment as the basic approach to address the B&R investment and financing issues.

3.2.1. Pursuing innovation and integration

To build a new investment and financing system for the BRI, China should strengthen policy coordination of all countries involved in the initiative; make great efforts to improve top-level design; stimulate the enthusiasm of enterprises and financial institutions; take opinions of all related departments, market players and financial institutions into consideration; compare China's national rules and practices with international rules and standards on a case-by-case basis; and blend with international rules in an innovative way factoring in specific national conditions, laws, cultures and social environment of other BRI countries and interests of all parties.

3.2.2. Seeking common ground while respecting differences

When taking part in the B&R investment and financing projects, Chinese enterprises and financial institutions should follow the principles of "seeking common ground while respecting differences, participating on an equal footing, sharing interests and risks". All countries, regardless of their size and national strength, should negotiate on an equal footing; Chinese market players' participation in investment and financing is not to unilaterally inject growth momentum into the beneficiary countries, but to realize benefit sharing in the project construction; risks arising from project operation should not be borne by China alone but be shared by all; as long as it is conducive to the development of countries involved in the BRI, all parties should try to negotiate and compromise.

3.2.3. Adopting differentiated measures

Adopting differentiated measures refers to taking varied steps based on an objective evaluation of China's existing capabilities to actively initiate, innovatively integrate into and participate in the revision of some investment and financing rules.

The first step is to take the initiative to develop a set of international rules to show the world Chinese wisdom and Chinese solutions. The second is to take the initiative to integrate into a number of international rules for better participation in international governance. The third is to take the initiative to innovatively improve an array of rules so that most countries are ready to accept them.

3.2.4. Tailor-making to local conditions

China should not wait passively or be shy of challenges encountered in clearing the Belt and Road investment and financing obstacles, but actively seek solutions in view of local conditions.

To sum up, to improve the investment and financing of the BRI, China should reform and innovate the existing credit rules and management and control systems, ameliorate and perfect the existing investment protection system and mechanism, strengthen the investment and financing risk assessment and early warning system, innovatively integrate into and change the current international debt default and bailout mechanisms, toughen the fight against corruption and commercial bribery, enhance the transparency of investment and financing information, and promote the internationalization of the renminbi.

4 Reforming existing credit rules for the Belt and Road Initiative

There still exists a gap between the "open and sharing" ideas and rules of Chinese financial institutions on financing terms, interest rates, China's content, and approval. It is thus necessary to reform and innovate existing financing systems and rules for the following two reasons: first, enhancing the international competitiveness of Chinese capital and allowing BRI projects to use more Chinese capital; and second, enabling Chinese capital and capital of countries in Europe and North America to contribute jointly to the B&R investment and financing.

4.1. A mechanism in which financial institutions and enterprises share benefits to reduce costs

A multi-pronged approach is applied to study how to lower the high costs of Chinese financial institutions' foreign currency lending. The first involves exploring financing in the international financial market with sovereign credit and then relending the money to domestic financial institutions (government finance can ask financial institutions to pay a small amount of guarantee fees) to lower the foreign currency loan costs of financial institutions without sovereign rating. The second involves exploring the model in which the foreign exchange administration grants entrusted loans to a financial institution at a low interest rate first, then the financial institution lends to an enterprise at a low interest rate and finally the enterprise transfers part of its profits to the foreign exchange administration after becoming profitable. In this way, national foreign exchange reserves can generate income, and enterprises' investment in the Belt and Road Initiative is facilitated as well. The third is exploring the benefit flow mechanism between financial institutions and enterprises. By introducing structured loan instruments, such as loan agreements with options or valuation adjustment mechanism (VAM) agreements, financial institutions are encouraged to finance enterprises at a low interest rate, and companies will provide part of their profits to financial institutions based on settlements.

4.2. Developing an export credit policy combining "national content" and "national interests"

Based on the "national content" policy, some countries have suggested the "national interests" principle in recent years. This proposal is adapting to the trends of global economy.

China can apply the "national interests" principle to officially supported export credits while relaxing the requirement on national content to encourage Chinese enterprises to participate in global competition and back Chinese enterprises to process or purchase more "cost-effective" goods from all over the world to serve the BRI and follow the "national interests" principle more in financing and insurance policies.

4.3. Raising the percentage of financing in renminbi or local currency and extending credit terms

Great efforts should be made to study the ways and methods of expanding the use of renminbi or local currency in the B&R investment and financing so as to gradually reduce dependence on the US dollar.

To address the current short financing period, China should, on the basis of comprehensively studying international popular practices, adjust the maturity structure of the country's export credits or assistance, and allow longer repayment terms for some projects involving big loan amounts and long payback periods to ensure borrowing countries have enough time to develop their economies and generate profits and strike a balance between loan repayment and local economic development. This will benefit the long-term development of the BRI much more.

4.4. Strengthening industry guidance and improving credit supervisory and assessment system

Chinese supervisors and banks should earnestly study the guarantee policy on bank credit business, attach importance to cash flows of projects and allow banks to bear part of the risks, without single-minded pursuit of guarantees with collateral or full coverage of risks with guarantee. They can strengthen and enhance banks' risk control capabilities. Due to handling of risks, banks will place a higher premium on customer screening and enhanced due diligence before lending, and monitor and manage the loan drawdown, repayment and execution more responsibly during and after lending.

In addition, from the perspective of supervision, assessment and incentives, Chinese investors and financial institutions should be encouraged to use the project financing method in BRI projects more. The biggest characteristic of project financing is that the repayment mainly comes from cash flows arising from the projects themselves, and its essence lies in allocating risks to the most suitable bearers. Project financing ties the parties together to form a community of shared interests. This can bring more returns to financing banks, expose initiators to less risks and increase the certainty of projects' future returns.

4.5. Innovate business models to ease the financial stress of government finance and initiators

Currently, many infrastructure projects under the BRI raise money in the simple and efficient form of sovereign borrowings. But sovereign borrowings have shortcomings, too. Since the repayment relies totally on sovereign credit, mismanagement will give rise to sovereign default and affect follow-up projects, thus harming the sustainability of the BRI. Moreover, as the decisions on sovereign borrowing projects are carried out by government departments, those involved in decision-making are a small group of people without the needed experience. Therefore this can damage the scientific nature of decisions made, and sometimes leads to launch of unnecessary or thoughtless projects because of commercial bribery.

Currently, many countries are vigorously promoting the public-private partnership (PPP) model and the build-operate-transfer (BOT) model. Under both models, the government and the private sector reach a concession agreement based on the purchase and provision of related products and services. The private sector is responsible for financing, as well as project building and operation, while government departments provide policy and related support, including being responsible for the outputs of purchased projects, thereby forming a partnership which expands common interests, shares risks and engages in cooperation all the way. PPP/BOT reflects higher economic/time efficiency, which can stimulate investment in infrastructure projects, improve the financial soundness of both public and private sectors, achieve long-term planning and improve the public sector's image.

4.6. Increasing the use of syndicated loans and vigorously promoting co-insurance and reinsurance

There is a big problem in the current financing system: a very large single project needs to borrow hundreds of millions or even billions of US dollars. One or two Chinese banks may lend money to the project, but they are unwilling or unable to organize international syndication, leading to excessive concentration of risks in Chinese financial institutions. International financial institutions, meanwhile, usually arrange international syndicated loans, with multiple participants sharing risks reasonably and controlling risks jointly. What's more, international banks generally try to invite multilateral financial institutions (e.g. the World Bank, the Multilateral Investment Guarantee Agency (MIGA), ADB and AIDB). Their engagement can significantly reduce project risks.

In regard to policy-related export credit insurance, some medium- and long-term insurance projects are also exclusively underwritten by SINOSURE, without reinsurance or co-insurance arrangements made with foreign peers. China should learn from international practices and engage in reinsurance or co-insurance arrangements with foreign insurers. For some projects under the BRI, exporters from developed Western countries serve as turnkey contractors, but they may subcontract part of equipment supply or project construction to a Chinese company. In this case, the Western country's ECA provides corresponding medium- and long-term credit insurance. For the purpose of controlling and diversifying risks, the ECA generally expects SINOSURE to provide insurance for the work done by the Chinese subcontractor.

So, relevant Chinese financial institutions and insurance companies should vigorously promote international syndicated loans, as well as reinsurance and co-insurance with reference to the practices of foreign peers. Through cooperation with a wider range of parties, they can establish relationships with more stakeholders to help diversify and reduce risks and improve international image and competitiveness, thus being in a better position to serve the B&R investment and financing activities.

5 Optimizing the Belt and Road investment protection and dispute settlement mechanisms

The sustainable development of the Belt and Road Initiative calls for all types of entities in all countries to increase investment in and financing for nations involved in the initiative. In particular, equity investment can come into bigger play. For one thing, it can avoid aggravating the debt burden on invested countries and lessen their financial strain; for the other, it can meet the actual needs of countries from a longerterm and more sustainable perspective, support the development of the invested countries' real economy, accelerate their industrialization process, enhance their sustainable development capabilities and ultimately allow these economic development outcomes to benefit local people and embark on the road of common development.

How to ensure the security of various types of investments by China and other countries in countries involved in the Belt and Road Initiative has become a big concern in encouraging and attracting investors. Bilateral investment protection agreements ("BIPAs") are the most important investment regulation, protection, and promotion tool in the world. To resolve investment disputes, the international community has gradually put in place a mechanism based on arbitration, which has the advantages of rapidness, confidentiality and autonomy.

5.1. China's cooperation with B&R countries in equity investment

Direct equity investment across borders is key and central to China's economic cooperation with other countries involved in the Belt and Road Initiative. The focus of cooperation includes connectivity of infrastructure and facilities, energy resource cooperation, industrial park construction and advantageous capacity cooperation. From 2014 to September 2019, China invested more than US$100 billion in countries involved in the BRI. The invested industries are becoming increasingly diversified, and M&A activities remain brisk. It is expected that China's direct investment in BRI countries will rise significantly and bring even broader prospects for cooperation.

Presently, China mainly increases investment in countries involved in the BRI through policy guidance or development-oriented funds, market entities' spontaneous investment and overseas economic and trade cooperation zones. By channeling long-term equity funds, China has made long-term commitments to the BRI.

5.1.1. Guidance by policy or development-oriented funds

Policy and development funds mainly include the Silk Road Fund, China-Africa Development Fund, China-CEEC Fund and China-CEEC Investment Cooperation Fund. Like the seed capital, they play a crucial guiding role in the Belt and Road investment.

5.1.2. Equity investment by market entities

Market entities in China have made handsome equity investment along the Belt and Road, mostly in capital-intensive industries such as electricity, energy, oil and gas, and mining, and a few in capacity cooperation and manufacturing.

5.1.3. Large amount equity investment through overseas economic and trade cooperation zones

According to the Ministry of Commerce of China, as of September 2018, Chinese enterprises had invested US$36.63 billion cumulatively in 113 cooperation zones still under construction in 46 countries, with 4,663 enterprises already settled in those zones. Specifically, Chinese companies invested US$30.45 billion in 82 cooperation zones which were home to 4,098 companies.

5.2. Multi-tiered investment protection and dispute settlement mechanisms

5.2.1. BIPAs

Since the 1990s, bilateral investment protection agreements (BIPAs) have gradually become the main pillar of the legal framework for international investment. As of the end of 2016, there were 3,304 international investment protection agreements worldwide,[1] including 2,946 BIPAs, marking an increasingly larger network of BIPAs.

Generally speaking, BIPAs contain terms and conditions on investment definition, national treatment, most-favored-nation treatment, fair and equitable treatment, expropriation compensation standards, host country's exchange restrictions, host country's defaults and international arbitration. These terms and conditions define the form, content, treatment, relief measures and dispute settlement of the investments. Investors of a country are entitled to compensation if their investments in another country have been treated unfairly as stipulated in the agreements.

So far, China has signed BIPAs with 130 countries,[2] including 102 nations where BIPAs were already in force.

5.2.2. Investment protection in FTAs

Free trade agreements (FTAs) include bilateral and multilateral ones. The sections on investment in FTAs are roughly the same as those in BIPAs.

Taking the FTA signed between China and Maldives in December 2017 as an example, the investment chapter says both parties should give high-level investment protection to the other party, and incorporates terms on expropriation compensations, minimum treatment standards, transfer and so on, as well as national treatment and most-favored-nation treatment for the phase after access is provided to each other; the chapter sets forth such exceptions as financial prudential measures, fundamental security and confidential information so as to protect the policy space for foreign fund management by the government, and incorporates the comprehensive mechanism for settlement of disputes between investors and the state to provide the full right guarantee and remedy approach for investors of both parties.

In September 2018, China and Mauritius announced the conclusion of negotiations on a free trade agreement, the first FTA between China and an African country.

China has conducted multiple rounds of negotiations on the Regional Comprehensive Economic Partnership Agreement (RCEP) with 16 countries in the Asia-Pacific, including ten ASEAN members, Japan, South Korea, Australia, New Zealand and India. They have held extensive discussions on goods, services, investments, rules of origin, customs procedures and trade facilitation, trade remedies, finance, telecommunications, intellectual property rights, e-commerce and other areas. China has also been in FTA negotiations with more than a dozen countries and regions, including Panama, Nepal and Palestine.

5.2.3. *Investment dispute settlement mechanisms*

Disputes in international investment that occur between investors (commercial entities) and cannot be resolved through negotiation, settlement or conciliation often have to go through legal proceedings or arbitration. However, if the proceedings happen in a court of a party's homeland, the other party will face the real issue of judicial bias. Therefore, investors in cross-border investment usually avoid agreeing to institute legal proceedings with the courts of a party's homeland. But a third country's court may refuse to accept the case, and judgment may be unenforceable in the country where the losing party and its property are located.

Due to the above-mentioned shortcomings of court proceedings, more and more investors resort to international arbitration which has the characteristics of confidentiality, final ruling and expert judgment. International commercial arbitration is currently the most widely used method to settle commercial disputes, and also one of the most effective and fair dispute settlement methods. In terms of which arbitration institutions to choose, investors usually pick the International Court of Arbitration of the International Chamber of Commerce (ICC), the London Court of International Arbitrationor the Arbitration Institute of the Stockholm Chamber of Commerce, among others, which are quite experienced and enjoy high reputation around the world.

Disputes or conflicts between foreign investors and host governments can be settled in many different ways, including filing with administrative and judicial authorities in the host country, ad hoc arbitration, institutional arbitration and international arbitration. But the above-mentioned ways are localized in procedures and substantive law applications vary. In comparison, the International Centre for Settlement of Investment Disputes (ICSID) is an arbitration institution established under the World Bank by the Convention on the Settlement of Investment Disputes between States and Nationals of Other States (the "Washington Convention"). Without localized arbitration rules, law applications and enforcement of awards, ICSID has appeared in international treaties containing investment rules as a recommended way of resolving investment disputes. Furthermore, seen from the past arbitrations of ICSID, the investors won in many cases it handles because the host countries' law and policy changes constituted a violation of international treaty obligations. Therefore, based on system design and practices, ICSID is a top pick by foreign investors for dispute settlement.

5.2.3.1. *The Washington Convention and ICSID*

The Washington Convention provides a forum for investor–state dispute settlement for the first time, makes it possible to resolve the disputes between host states and foreign investors through international arbitration on the sphere of international laws, maintains a careful balance between the interests of investors and host states and offers a good environment for international investment. The Washington Convention is a treaty ratified by 154 Contracting States (by August 2018). In eight countries, namely, Russia, Thailand, Belize, Dominica, Guinea-Bissau, Kyrgyzstan, Namibia, and Ethiopia, they have signed the Convention, but it has not yet entered into force there. China ratified the Washington Convention in 1992 and declared that in accordance with Article 25.4 of the Convention, the country only considers submitting expropriation and nationalization compensations to the jurisdiction of ICSID.

After the Washington Convention entered into force, arbitration has witnessed unprecedented advances as a way to resolve international investment disputes. The status of ICSID has been continuously consolidated and elevated. ICSID is an independent, depoliticized and non-localized forum without administrative or judicial interventions from host states or countries where investors are located. And the Washington Convention entitles each member state to designate up to four persons to the panel of arbitrators and up to four persons to the panel of conciliators. More and more BIPAs and multilateral/regional treaties have made ICSID an important option for the settlement of international investment disputes. As of the end of 2017, ICSID administered 650 cases, including 587 arbitration cases and the rest for conciliation. Most of these cases were submitted to ICSID for arbitration in accordance with the arbitration provisions set forth in the BIPAs and investment contracts signed by and between host governments and foreign investors' countries. Today, ICSID administers 70% of all known international investment proceedings.

5.2.3.2. *The New York Convention*

Relative to legal proceedings, the biggest advantage of arbitration is the extraterritorial enforcement of awards. The Convention on the Recognition and Enforcement of Foreign Arbitral Awards, also known as theNew York Convention, is the most important convention in the international arbitration sector. It focuses on addressing the recognition and enforcement by courts of contracting states of arbitral awards made in other contracting states. To date, 156 countries and regions, including the vast majority of countries involved in the BRI, have acceded to the New York Convention.

Thanks to the New York Convention, the recognition and enforcement of foreign and non-domestic arbitral awards in various countries have made satisfactory progress, and such rulings are not discriminated against. Moreover, arbitration is often heard by arbitrators in a neutral third country's arbitration institution designated by the parties, which greatly reduces the possible bias of the tribunal or that one party might interfere with the trial by improper means, thus helping safeguard justice and impartiality. In this sense, agreeing to submit a dispute to international arbitration is often the best option for the parties. However, it should be noted that a few countries involved in the BRI are not parties to the New York Convention, and some other countries do not have mature arbitration systems, or their arbitration systems go against the recognition and enforcement of arbitral awards. It is thus necessary to tailor-make dispute settlement clauses to the different arbitration systems in different countries.

5.2.3.3. *China's dispute settlement mechanisms*

As the BRI forges ahead, China is attaching increasing importance to the building of cross-border investment dispute settlement mechanisms in respect to national policy, judicial decision and arbitration institution. The country has taken a multi-pronged approach to play a due role in resolving the disputes involving Chinese parties and providing a more transparent and foreseeable domestic platform for its own dispute settlement.

The Several Opinions on Providing Judicial Services and Safeguards for the Belt and Road Initiative by People's Courts issued by the Supreme People's Court in 2015 permits China's courts to grant legal reciprocity to other countries involved in the initiative. As there is no binding treaty, litigants must seek to enforce foreign judgments in China on the basis of reciprocity. Since 2015, some foreign judgments have been enforced in China either through a bilateral treaty or reciprocity. In 2015, the Wuhan Intermediate People's Court enforced the judgment made by the Los Angeles Superior Court concerning *Liu Li v. Tao Li and Tong Wu* (the "Liu Li Case"). It was the first time that a Chinese court had recognized and enforced a foreign judgment on the reciprocity principle. The Wuhan Court referred to the case of *Hubei Gezhouba Sanlian Indus. Co. v. Robinson Helicopter Co.*, in which the US District Court for the Central District of California enforced the rulings of the

Higher People's Court of Hubei Province in the United States. In the case of *Kolmar Group AG v. Jiangsu Textile Industry Import and Export Corporation*, the Nanjing Intermediate People's Court recognized and enforced a judgment from the Singapore High Court on the grounds that *de facto* reciprocity had been previously established in Singapore, citing an earlier Singapore court decision (*Giant Light Metal Technology (Kunshan) Co., Ltd v. Aksa Far East Pte Ltd*) in which the High Court of Singapore recognized and enforced a civil judgment rendered by the Suzhou Intermediate People's Court in Jiangsu Province. The practice of reciprocity facilitates the settlement of disputes in the BRI through filing lawsuits with courts.

The *Opinions Concerning the Establishment of the Belt And Road International Commercial Dispute Resolution Mechanism and Institutions* China issued in January 2018 points out that the following principles should be complied with in respect of the establishment of the Belt and Road international commercial dispute resolution mechanism and institutions: the principle of wide consultation, joint contribution and shared benefits; the principle of impartiality, efficiency and convenience; the principle of party autonomy; and the principle of resolving disputes in diverse ways. According to the *Opinions*, and drawing on the experiences of the Singapore International Commercial Court and the Dubai International Financial Centre Courts, in June 2018, the Supreme People's Court of China established the First International Commercial Court in Shenzhen, Guangdong Province, and the Second International Commercial Court in Xi'an, Shaanxi Province. Later, it appointed eight judges and set up the International Commercial Expert Committee, which appointed the first group of 32 experts (over 50% were foreigners) in August.

Chinese arbitration institutions are paying increasing attention to the building of international investment arbitration mechanisms. The International Investment Arbitration Rules of the China International Economic and Trade Arbitration Commission ("CIETAC Investment Arbitration Rules") came into force on October 1, 2017. The CIETAC Investment Arbitration Rules, together with the CIETAC Investment Dispute Settlement Center (IDSC) in Beijing, are aimed at filling the gap of China in the international investment arbitration field. For the first time China has tried to settle international investment disputes by establishing an arbitration institution. The CIETAC Investment Arbitration Rules and IDSC make available alternatives for resolving investor–state disputes apart from traditional choices such as ICSID, the UNCITRAL Arbitration Rules and the ICC International Court of Arbitration.

Wuhan Arbitration Commission set up the Belt and Road (China) Arbitration Court in October 2016, the first professional arbitration court serving the BRI. The court mainly accepts disputes or conflicts arising from construction projects and commercial projects under the BRI, and dedicates itself to properly handling disputes of Chinese companies in conducting investment, engineering contracting and EPC/ subcontracting outside China.

The Supreme People's Court of China is also increasing awareness of the enforcement of foreign-related arbitration cases in China. In December 2017, the Supreme People's Court released the *Relevant Provisions on Issues Concerning Applications for Approval of Arbitration Cases under Judicial Review* and the *Provisions on Several Issues Concerning Deciding Cases of Arbitration-Related Judicial Review* (collectively referred to as the "Provisions"). Entering into force on January 1, 2018, the Provisions address the judicial review of arbitration cases. According to the Provisions, if the arbitration agreement is to be determined as invalid, the application of recognition and enforcement of the arbitration award is to be rejected or the arbitral ruling is to be set aside, then the court which accepts the case shall report the case to the higher court within the same jurisdiction for approval. If the higher court agrees with the lower court's opinion, it shall report the case to the Supreme People's Court for further approval. The Supreme People's Court has the decision-making power to confirm the ruling on the invalidity/refusal/setting aside. For foreign-related arbitration cases, or for mainland arbitration cases in which the domiciles of the parties are located in different provinces or the ground for refusing enforcement or setting aside the arbitral awards is the violation of public interests, they shall be submitted to the Supreme People's Court for approval. The decision-making power of the judicial review related to mainland cases without involving public interests shall be exercised by the Higher People's Court in the jurisdiction where application is filed.

5.3. Inadequate protection from existing investment protection agreements and dispute settlement mechanisms

5.3.1. *Imperfections in China's talks on and signing of investment protection agreements*

Relative to the construction requirements of the B&R and the strong overseas investment needs of various enterprises, there are still imperfections in China's talks on and signing of BIPAs.

First, China has not signed BIPAs with some countries, or signed agreements which have not become effective officially. So far, China has only signed BIPAs with 130 countries, including 102 agreements in force. China has signed BIPAs/FTAs with 56/11 countries involved in the BRI. It has not discussed or signed BIPAs with, for instance, Iraq, Palestine, Afghanistan, Maldives, Nepal, Bhutan and Montenegro, or the signed ones, such as those with Brunei, Jordan, Bangladesh and Bosnia and Herzegovina, have not yet entered into force.

Second, BIPA provisions are incomplete. Right now, overseas investment activities of Chinese enterprises have shown new characteristics in invested industries, investment scales, investment destinations and so on. In addition, there are new changes in the international landscape. So, the provisions of original BIPAs do not adapt to new investment needs because of poorly defined "investor" and "investment", "post-access" provisions restricting investment, unclear indirect expropriation provisions and limited scope of arbitrable matters.

Third, the coexistence of various investment agreements easily leads to legal conflicts. China has already signed BIPAs with Japan and South Korea, but the three countries concluded a trilateral investment protection agreement in 2012 while the previous BIPAs are still in effect. This is also the case with the China–ASEAN investment protection agreement. The overlapping of investment protection agreements will possibly lead to a large number of legal conflicts, making it more difficult for governments to seek multilateral coordination for investment.

5.3.2. *BRI countries to strengthen investment protection and dispute settlement*

Based on an in-depth analysis of investment protection by countries involved in the BRI, we believe these nations are trying their best to attract foreign capital and thus paying attention to holding discussions and signing investment protection agreements with other countries. However, the investment protection efforts remain limited, and the dispute settlement mechanisms still have defects.

First, some countries have unilaterally terminated BIPAs, impairing the sustainability of investment protection rules.

Second, some BIPAs have conflicts with the laws of host countries or they have lacunae, making it impossible to bring the role of investment protection and international arbitration mechanisms in some projects into full play.

Nowadays, many Chinese energy and infrastructure companies are going global to participate in foreign PPP projects. Some countries have standardized PPP contracts in accordance with law to attract investment. This can benefit China a lot. However, the fact that host countries' laws are not coherent with BIPAs may result in Chinese companies failing to protect their own legitimate rights and interests based on BIPAs when they take part in investing activities.

5.4. Strengthening and improving investment protection rules and dispute settlement mechanisms

5.4.1. *Signing, amending or renegotiating on BIPAs*

The absence of BIPA is not conducive to bilateral investment under the BRI. Even if there is a BIPA, it is necessary to revise the terms and conditions as time goes by and bilateral relations evolve. China signed BIPAs with many countries in the last century, when the country mainly acted as the "host country" of foreign investment. So BIPAs then were often designed for the purpose of favoring the host country, and they might go against the investors in some cases. For example, under the dispute settlement mechanism in the China–UAE BIPA which was signed in 1993, Chinese investors can only submit disputes related to the amount of compensation or disputes agreed by the parties to treaty arbitration for international arbitration, while submitting other investment disputes to local administrative organ in the UAE for complaint or to local court for action. We can see from this example that, even if there is an effective investment protection agreement between China and a host country, the agreement may not accommodate to the actual requirements of China's role change to the source of investment under the BRI. For this reason, China should amend or re-sign such agreements based on China's actual conditions and the needs of the BRI, with a particular emphasis on investor protection.

It is imperative to promote the signing of such agreements between China and countries that have not yet signed BIPAs, such as Iraq, Palestine, Afghanistan, Maldives, Nepal, Bhutan and Montenegro. China should push the BIPAs signed with Brunei, Jordan, Bangladesh and Bosnia and Herzegovina to enter into force as quickly as possible or renegotiate if necessary. Besides, as the developing country that attracts the most foreign investment and invests the largest in the rest of the world, China has not yet signed a BIPA with the United States, which tops the world in terms of foreign investment attracted and made. China and the European Union started negotiations on an investment agreement in 2013, and both sides should strengthen their negotiation efforts.

5.4.2. Making more efforts on multilateral trade and investment protection agreement talks

The BRI involves a lot of countries. Therefore, the multilateral investment cooperation mechanism should be strengthened in parallel with seeking progress in BIPAs. We propose to study the possibility of discussing and signing a multilateral investment protection agreement applicable to all nations involved in the initiative with reference to the North American Free Trade Agreement, the Agreement on Dispute Settlement Mechanism of the Framework Agreement on Comprehensive Economic Cooperation between China and ASEAN, and the Agreement on Trade in Goods of the Framework Agreement on Comprehensive Economic Cooperation between China and ASEAN, among others, in order to encourage BRI countries to strengthen mutual investment and trade and at the same time attract companies in countries not along the Belt and Road to invest in B&R nations.

To address the problem that both bilateral and multilateral investment agreements between China and some countries/regions are all in force, China needs to improve bilateral/multilateral collaboration and minimize the conflicts among such agreements to eliminate potential legal disputes. Besides, China should cancel the declaration of only considering submitting disputes over compensation resulting from expropriation and nationalization to the jurisdiction of ICSID made on accession to the Washington Convention, and the "commercial reservation" made on joining the New York Convention. (Pursuant to the commercial reservation, China applies the Convention only to disputes arising from contractual and non-contractual commercial legal relations under Chinese law. The so-called contractual and non-contractual commercial legal relations refer specifically to economic rights and obligations arising from contracts, torts or in accordance with relevant legal provisions, such as the sale of goods, lease of property, engineering contracting, processing contracts, insurance, and credit and labor services, but exclude disputes between foreign investors and host governments.)

5.4.3. Improving the overseas investment comprehensive protection framework on the basis of investment protection agreements

The agreement on comprehensive protection of overseas investment consists of three tiers: first, all types of investment protection agreements; second, overseas investment insurance systems; and third, provision of security, legal and other aids (e.g. consular protection, overseas security, mutual legal assistance) to enterprises by all departments together. Overseas investment insurance is a policy insurance tool set up by governments to promote capital export and protect the investment of domestic investors in host countries. It insures against such risks as expropriation, government default, exchange restriction, war and political upheavals. In the event of such risks, the insurer (generally the official agency of the country) will compensate the investors and collect damages from the host country via subrogation. Countries without overseas investment insurance ought to put it in place quickly. Countries like China which has such insurance in place but has not yet made it into law should accelerate the legislative process, and study and formulate the Overseas Investment Insurance Law or the Export Credit Insurance Law (incorporate overseas investment insurance into it). Besides, China should gradually define the subrogation of Chinese overseas investment insurance agency, which is entitled to negotiate and collect damages on behalf of the Chinese government.

5.4.4. *Spurring the building of a mechanism for settling disputes arising from the Belt and Road Initiative*

5.4.4.1. Signing the Convention on Choice of Court Agreements to promote the recognition and enforcement of judgments by civil and commercial courts

On September 12, 2017, China signed the Hague Convention on Choice of Court Agreements (the "Convention"), which was adopted by the Hague Conference on Private International Law on June 30, 2005, and became effective on October 1, 2015. The Convention has 30 contracting states now. It ensures the effectiveness of exclusive choice of court agreements between parties to civil and commercial cases and the recognition and enforcement of judgments resulting from proceedings based on such agreements. According to the Convention, a court of a contracting state must respect the exclusive jurisdiction clause in the commercial agreement and facilitate the jurisdiction of other contracting states' courts through suspending proceedings in one's own country. The Convention provides that a contracting state must recognize and enforce the judgments given by courts of other contracting states.

The Convention has 30 contracting states only, far less than 150 members of the Washington Convention and the New York Convention, which govern arbitration. The United States has not approved the Convention since becoming a signatory in 2009. Plus, the application scope of the Convention excludes many conditions. The Convention shall not apply to the following matters: employment contracts; the status and legal capacity of natural persons; insolvency matters; the carriage of passengers and goods; marine affairs; anti-trust (competition) matters; claims for personal injury brought by or on behalf of natural persons; tort or delict claims for damage to tangible property that do not arise from a contractual relationship; rights in rem in immovable property, and tenancies of immovable property; and infringement of intellectual property rights other than copyright and related rights.

Although the place and scope the Convention applies to are still relatively limited, the legal basis it provides for recognition and enforcement of foreign judgments acts a good platform for resolving disputes arising from the BRI, which can strengthen China's international cooperation in recognizing foreign judicial decisions and promote the BRI-related disputes to be better resolved through court hearing.

5.4.4.2. *Continuously improving arbitrations and arbitration effectiveness*

China has established two international commercial courts in Shenzhen and Xi'an, the Belt and Road (China) Arbitration Court under the Wuhan Arbitration Commission, the Shanghai Belt and Road International Arbitration Center, and other special courts and arbitration bodies to handle the settlement of disputes arising from the BRI. Based on this, China can jointly initiate and set up the Belt and Road International Investment Dispute Settlement Center with other countries involved in the initiative, and define the center's arbitration and enforcement rules with reference to the settings of ICSID. Disputes between investors, between investors and states, and between states can be submitted to the center. China can persuade all countries that accept and endorse the BRI to explicitly support the center's arbitrations and ensure that the arbitral rulings are recognized and enforced by the courts of all member states.

China should strongly support the establishment of a joint arbitration mechanism between Chinese arbitration institutions and arbitration institutions in other countries involved in the BRI, and encourage Chinese law firms to participate in dispute resolution if conditions permit and request arbitration institutions to employ qualified Chinese experts to be members, arbitrators or mediators. Chinese courts should allow enforcement of foreign arbitration and mediation documents through judicial recognition. Countries involved in the BRI should put in place a mechanism for mutually recognizing arbitral awards.

A country's legal department should grant arbitration institutions dealing with BRI-related disputes powers in property preservation, evidence preservation and so on, and actively enforce arbitral rulings on the basis of facilitating and accelerating judicial review.

China should call on B&R countries that have not yet acceded to the New York Convention and the Washington Convention to do so quickly.

5.4.4.3. *Investors to make good use of ICSID's dispute settlement mechanism*

As ICSID provides neutral international mediation and arbitration procedures, Chinese companies may consider establishing the holding companies of their special purpose vehicles in countries that have signed an investment protection agreement containing the ICSID arbitration-based dispute settlement mechanism with host countries, when designing overseas investment structure.

Notes

1 Website of the United Nations Conference on Trade and Development (http://investmentpolicyhub.unctad.org)
2 Website of the Ministry of Commerce (http://hzs.mofcom.gov.cn)

6 Strengthening the Belt and Road investment and financing risk assessment and early warning

So far, many countries involved in the Belt and Road Initiative have not put in place a mechanism for ensuring investment and financing. Besides, they do not have a sound investment and financing risk assessment and early warning system, and lack understanding of systematic risks. Therefore, timely analyzing issues existing in risk assessment and early warning, building a holistic and coordinated mechanism for ensuring investment and financing, covering B&R nations with a risk assessment and early warning system and enhancing financial institutions' risk identification, management and control capabilities are of vital importance to the B&R investment and financing work.

6.1. Imperfections in B&R investment and financing risk assessment and early warning

6.1.1. Absence of mechanism for ensuring investment and financing

Currently, almost all countries involved in the Belt and Road Initiative do not have a task force on ensuring investment and financing for economic cooperation under the BRI, and they fail to consider how to provide basic support for investment and financing risk assessment and early warning from the perspective of establishing an agency to support and serve investment and financing in a regulated, systematic and ongoing way. The mechanism for ensuring investment in and financing for countries involved in the BRI should be made a long-term effective mechanism for boosting project investment and financing, with particular emphasis on guarantees based on investment and financing risk assessment service and support, targets, institutional design and implementation steps. Although many agencies can provide support and guarantees, their definition of responsibilities and positioning are not clear, and the content of their work does not take into account the actual requirements of addressing B&R investment and financing risks.

6.1.2. Incomplete risk assessment and early warning system

First, the B&R risk assessment framework is uncertain. It is recognized by all that overall risk level of countries involved in the BRI is high, but no consensus has been reached on the dimensions, major indicators and methods of risk assessment. Besides, the risk assessment reports published by some institutions are inconsistent and impractical, and the assessment conclusions are contradictory. Second, there is no risk assessment system from the BRI's perspective. Under the existing risk assessment framework of the Western world, some countries involved in the BRI are exposed to extremely high risks; so other nations are wary of investing in these nations. But this will obviously deprive these high-risk countries of the rights to pursue socioeconomic progress, and it runs counter to the aspirations of the initiative for wide consultation, joint contribution and shared benefits. Multinationals, financial institutions and academic research institutions need to join hands to study how to scientifically assess the country, industry and buyer (business) risks in economic cooperation of B&R countries. Second, information and data support is relatively behind the curve, and there is no big data and data mining-based risk database. For example, the data on export credit volume and foreign currency loan scale and so on of B&R projects are inconsistent, and the authoritative statistics on investment in and financing for countries involved in the initiative are incomplete. All these problems are stumbling blocks to countries, financial institutions and enterprises when they try to perform early warning modeling through basic information analysis and on this basis to make scientific and reasonable risk perceptions.

6.1.3. Insufficient assessment and understanding of country and systematic risks

Because the overall risk level of countries involved in the BRI is relatively high, their investment and financing, particularly large investment projects in high-risk B&R nations, must not only consider micro-business factors but also take into account project-related macro-political, economic and investment factors. However, some companies do not incorporate country risk into the comprehensive risk management system or deem it an important factor in making investment and financing decisions. Once there is a country risk exposure, companies will find it impossible to bear it alone and may thus incur significant losses.

6.2. Building a new open and shared system for risk assessment and early warning

6.2.1. Creating a holistic and coordinated mechanism for ensuring investment and financing

6.2.1.1. Establishing an investment and financing promotion agency

Countries involved in the BRI may consider establishing an agency for promotion of investment in and financing for projects. The agency should be expected to have the following main responsibilities: first, bridging governments and enterprises, publishing government policies and interpretations of the latest documents and so on in time, and providing early warning of government policy risks; second, establishing legal, accounting, audit and other consulting service platforms for corporate investors, sorting out and identifying projects, inviting companies that pursue same economic interests to jointly participate in projects and enhancing their ability to jointly resist risks; and third, providing market forecasts and analyses, in particular, strengthening the monitoring and early warning of country risks, and forming a panoramic risk map of overseas investment and financing.

6.2.1.2. Promoting the building of a multi-level insurance and protection system

First, through bilateral and multilateral economic and trade mechanisms and institutional arrangements, China should strengthen strategic economic dialogue, communication and policy coordination with other countries involved in the BRI, and create a favorable environment for Chinese enterprises to invest abroad. Second, China should build a financial safety net in all the places involved in the initiative, strengthen cross-border supervisory policy coordination, establish a mechanism for cooperation with financial supervisors in other B&R countries and sign memoranda of understanding on bilateral supervisory cooperation. B&R countries can start from strengthening cooperation in micro-prudential financial supervision, building a regional financial cooperation platform and the like, and remain committed to improving economic and financial ties and the resilience of financial markets, as well as the abilities of regional financial markets to withstand the impact of external financial crises. A current priority is to encourage financial supervisors of countries in Central and Eastern Europe, the Middle East and North Africa, and South Asia to conclude a new memorandum of understanding. Third, drawing on the cooperation experience of the BRICS nations, countries involved in the BRI can put in place an insurance support system in which their insurers will co-provide commercial and policy risk protection for enterprises in order to encourage companies to increase project investment and financing efforts on the premise of averting risks properly and work together to control project risks.

6.2.1.3. Improving financial safety net and credit environment

First, China should establish a multi-level regional financial cooperation mechanism. On the basis of pooling experiences, China should further financial cooperation with Southeast Asia, South Asia and Central Asia, deepen cooperation with Central and Eastern Europe, and study and explore ways of cooperation with the Middle East and North Africa. Second, China should set up a "fund pool" with contributions from all B&R countries to resolve debt problems. A certain level of financial assistance should be provided to underdeveloped countries that are willing to repay but are insolvent. However, this kind of assistance should not be free, but in the form of preferential interest rates and tenors in a bid to spur sustainable economic and social progress of debt-defaulting countries. This "fund pool" can seek help from multilateral financial institutions and position itself as a platform for gradually becoming a multilateral debt default rescuer in the future. Third, China should strengthen cross-border cooperation in credit reporting. A unified and sound credit reporting system will expand the access of financial institutions to information and improve their utilization of information, allow financial institutions to have a clear picture of the operations and credit status of foreign enterprises at lower costs, encourage more high-quality companies to establish information communication channels with banks and move financial resources continuously to credible market entities, thereby optimizing credit resource allocations and reducing credit risks.

6.2.2. Putting in place a long-effective mechanism for risk assessment and early warning

First, China should value the importance of top-level design, leverage the coordination and communication between high-level officials of governments, accelerate the building of a scientific and reasonable risk assessment and early warning system for countries involved in the BRI and allow country risk management to function well in project investment and financing to serve the BRI. The country risk assessment and early warning system involving many different nations will engage a large number of government departments, research institutes, financial institutions and enterprises. Departments and institutions of different countries will act for varied purposes. Therefore, based on the organizational framework and tasks of OECD country risk analysis and research, a special research institute dedicated to the BRI consisting of all of the B&R countries should be established to conduct assessment and early warning of risks in these nations and also elsewhere in the world; country risk assessment reports and ratings should be published regularly as an important basis of perceiving and anticipating BRI project-related investment and financing risks.

Second, China should develop a country risk database covering the B&R project information and country risk information and so on, based on big data concept and technology. For one thing, the database development will be a basic task of country risk assessment and early warning for the fundamental purpose of helping countries involved in the BRI avert systematic risks and unbearable macro risks; for another, quantitative research and management of country risks will be empowered on the basis of all-round information and data collection and management, particularly providing more data on political and economic risks; and again, the aim would be to make the database become intelligent, i.e. getting risk assessment results in different scenarios and under different conditions with independent, objective risk analysis models.

Third, China should design a country risk assessment indicator system that serves the actual needs of project investment and financing. Country risk assessment needs to calibrate its approach by project, take into account practical needs and issues of the investment and financing projects, and satisfy the requirements of project risk management to the utmost in terms of assessment model indicator design.

6.2.3. Taking a holistic view on risk management and preparing advance measures for risk prevention, control and response

In the first place, enterprises should take a holistic view on risk management, build a specialized, indicator-based risk management system that suits the national conditions of host countries and their own development, incorporate country risk into the risk management and internal control system, fully assess the possible losses from country risk and sovereign credit risk factors, prepare in advance the measures for risk prevention and control, calculate the biggest risks they can tolerate before investing in or financing significant projects and explore how to build a differentiated risk management system specific to risk features of each country under a unified framework.

Second, enterprises should attach importance to systematic risks they are incapable of bearing. Although the probability of this type of risks is low, if it happens it will trap enterprises into tough times or even lead to bankruptcy. Therefore, companies should focus on geopolitical risk, war and political upheaval, nationalization and government default, terrorist attack, frequent regime change, slow economic growth, international imbalance of payments or imbalance between government revenue and expenditure, bad business environment and other hazards which can lead to unmanageable factors in business operations; thus, companies should take the risks listed seriously in project feasibility studies.

6.2.4. *Integrating policy-related financial resources and enhancing risk assessment and early warning capabilities*

The first need is to strengthen the collaboration of financial institutions, especially policy-oriented financial institutions, in investment and financing; give full play to the unique role of export credit insurance in driving project financing, increasing credit lines and reducing credit-related fees; optimize banks' loan approving and disbursing processes through export credit insurance, and establish a tripartite collaborative relationship among enterprises, banks and insurers; create conditions for the optimization and innovation of financing structure; and provide all types of companies comprehensive services blending financing support and risk reduction, in an effort to reduce potential risks at all levels and across various links.

The second need is to enable policy-oriented financial institutions related to foreign trade and investment to demonstrate strong information acquisition, claims recovery and risk analysis capabilities at the national, industrial and buyer levels. The policy role of export credit insurance should be brought into full play to help enterprises avoid and transfer systemic risks to the largest extent. That is, export credit insurance should function as the "risk taker" to help enterprises transfer and avoid unmanageable systemic risks, and leverage its powerful claims recovery channels to enhance the abilities to withstand the impact of external risks and the capacity for sustainable development.

The third need is to establish an independent foreign debt research and assessment mechanism involving financial institutions of different countries. Financial institutions and research institutes of nations involved in the BRI can jointly study the economic development and debt situation of each country; try to establish a new debt sustainability analysis framework; assess and review national governance, industrial structure and macro policies, and so on across the board; divide debt defaults into four categories (high, medium, low and unable to assess); and dynamically classify countries into the categories on an annual basis based on the debtor countries' foreign debt repayment ability and willingness, as well as the probability of defaulting on debts, so as to provide adequate basis for resolving debt defaults.

7 Building a new mechanism for resolving debt defaults in the Belt and Road investment and financing

7.1. Main issues in the debt default resolving mechanism

7.1.1. Insufficient bailouts for multilateral sovereign debt defaults

Under the prevailing international financial governance framework, the bailouts in the event of multilateral debt defaults take three forms mainly, namely short-term financial assistance, debt restructuring and debt relief. And there are four types of debt treatments according to collective action rules. First, some creditors set up organizations similar to "creditors' meetings" of their own accord, and launch non-mandatory negotiations in the form of institutional forums based on specific rules and procedures. Representative organizations include the Paris Club and the London Club, which focus on debt relief and debt restructuring, with a view to reaching an agreement on the basis of assessing debtor countries' solvency and willingness to repay debt; the second is ensuring the launch and implementation of negotiations and the protection of creditors by legal means based on the domestic laws of financially dominated countries, i.e. Collective Action Clauses (CACs) and Code of Conduct (CoC); third, international organizations bind the actions of all parties to debt restructuring, i.e. the Sovereign Debt Restructuring Mechanism (SDRM); and the fourth is seeking financial assistance from multilateral financial institutions such as the IMF and the World Bank, with extra emphasis placed on easing the liquidity crisis of debtor countries in the short and medium term and resolving debt problems of developing nations (mostly low-income nations in Asia, Africa and Latin America) under the Heavily Indebted Poor Country (HIPC) Initiative. The first and the fourth measures have proved to be the most effective, while the second and the third ones are mere theoretical explorations. We can regard the Paris Club an effective answer to the restrictive rules made by the IMF because the former prefers to address the sharing of benefits, powers and responsibilities, as well as the space of negotiations on all parties' rights and obligations through talks and consultations.

For countries involved in the Belt and Road Initiative, the existing mechanism for resolving multilateral sovereign debt defaults has the following shortcomings.

First, multilateral financial institutions and specialized non-government organizations are dominated by developed Western countries. Emerging market economies and developing nations do not have a voice and often find it difficult to press their reasonable demands at international financial institutions such as the IMF. In most cases, they can only passively accept whatever they are offered and are in a disadvantaged position in debt negotiations.

Second, according to the Paris Club, debt renegotiations are applied only for countries that clearly need debt relief, as evidenced by implementing an IMF program and its requisite economic policy conditionality. As a result, the IMF will possibly intervene in the political, economic and social governance of debtor countries by various means. If a country involved in the BRI accepts the IMF's assistance and the Paris Club's debt restructuring, it will have to say yes to Western countries and international financial institutions in which the West dominates in future economic development, thus sacrificing economic independence. Take the HIPC Initiative for example. The IMF and the World Bank (including the Paris Club) will monitor and assess debtor countries' economic and industrial adjustment policies, the government's fiscal and debt management capabilities and the effectiveness of economic reforms pursuant to relevant standards before reaching the decision point, between the decision point and the expected date for the completion point, and after the completion point. Especially when a debtor country fails to make satisfactory performance after the completion point, these organizations will propose to "correct" the debtor country's policies. These interventions will infringe on the sovereignty of debtor countries and damage their administration and policymaking capacity.

Third, debtor countries' debt management level is not fundamentally improved. Loan assistance of the IMF and debt restructuring of the Paris Club often forbid debtor countries from receiving loans from specific countries, and also set a limit on total foreign debt. This imposes restrictions on debtor countries to boost their economy via diversified financing and use of foreign capital, and hinders the normal foreign capital attraction and investing and financing activities of their governments and enterprises. Interventions in the sovereignty and policies of debtor countries have actually further reduced the willingness of governments to develop the economy and their debt management capabilities. Countries that do the bidding of these financial institutions for long may even lose their policymaking ability.

7.1.2. Imperfect bailouts of bilateral sovereign debt defaults

Due to the differences in trade, investment and other economic cooperation agreements signed by countries involved in the BRI, differences in economic strength of debtor countries and in their debt repayment willingness, it is difficult to handle bilateral debt defaults. Without recognized criteria and long-effective mechanisms, bailouts usually depend on bilateral talks and consultations. In a way, bilateral debt defaults among B&R countries are more about creditor countries' short-term financial assistance to debtor countries and some concessions to prior debts. Creditor countries often suffer a loss.

7.1.3. Limited resources for addressing non-sovereign debt defaults

Non-sovereign debt refers to the debt owed by for-profit commercial market entities to foreign market entities when they engage in economic cooperation. Government departments, public management departments under and strongly affiliated to government departments or SOEs are not obligated to and will not provide any guarantee for such debt. In general, creditors and debtors need to communicate on and resolve non-sovereign debt defaults in line with market principles, while the governments only provide assistance concerning bilateral agreements, communication channels, political effects and so on. Because countries involved in the BRI have a high risk level, weak economic and commercial foundation, and unsound investment and legal environment, in the event of default on long-term and a large amount of non-sovereign debt, commercial market entities and commercial communication channels alone will possibly not work. Besides, failure in generating expected returns in some projects after rollout and more investment in and financing for commercial projects will push up defaults, making it more necessary and urgent to resolve debt defaults.

7.2. Customizing a mechanism for resolving debt defaults of B&R countries

7.2.1. *Enhancing cooperation with multilateral organizations and protecting one's own legitimate rights and interests*

With the scale-up of B&R investment and financing, creditor and debtor countries are having more conflicts of interests or are even at odds with the IMF, the Paris Club and other multilateral organizations. Therefore, countries involved in the BRI need to make active responses, strengthen cooperation with these organizations and safeguard their economic interests. To address the disagreement with Western nations on debt issues, B&R countries should enhance negotiations and cooperation with the West, improve project transparency, tighten debt management, monitor debtors in real time, avoid excessive concentration of debts and manage and dispose of "offshore non-performing assets" with greater efforts.

Besides, they should view properly the scientific nature of the Paris Club's debt indicators for developing countries, and explore the significant project investment and financing models that are in line with their national conditions, respect the autonomous power of invested countries to seek economic development and take into account their debt sustainability. Drawing on the models, rules and practices of Western countries and multilateral organizations in resolving debt defaults, B&R countries should adopt debt restructuring and bailout defaulting countries.

7.2.2. *Factoring in multi-level reasonable demands of B&R countries*

The BRI involves vast markets and huge populations in many countries. Creditor and debtor nations must locate the area where they have common interests and consider the interest demands of the other party, especially the debt repayment willingness and solvency of debtor countries' governments and enterprises, as well as the sustainability of credit funds provided by creditor countries' governments and enterprises and their economic interest demands. Major creditor countries are recommended to fully consider the diversity of funding requirements of major debtor countries' governments and enterprises, and reasonably align the rhythm of project investment and financing with their market openness, financial environment and system, government's policy tendency and debt repayment willingness. In addition, two issues are worth mentioning: First, entities should not invest too much in a country that has a large demand for external funding, is vulnerable to a strong US dollar and fluctuations in international commodity prices, and thus has solvency issues, in order to avoid excessive country or country-industry concentrations. Second, look at the strategic significance of projects and investment and financing from a medium- and long-term perspective, and enhance short-term risk tolerance. When creditor and debt countries are unable to reconcile short-term interests, creditor countries may sacrifice some short-term interests for long-term benefits from the perspective of supporting economic growth and cultivating related industries and prospective market development of debtor countries.

7.2.3. *Exploring fresh models of debt restructuring and relief*

We suggest improving the influence of the AIDB, Silk Road Fund and BRICS New Development Bank with multi-country engagement, and leveraging their characteristics of contributing mainly to fund connectivity of B&R countries, developing and emerging market economies and BRICS member states; and try to develop the standards and models of resolving debt defaults which are jointly set by most B&R countries and are binding to a degree. For example, the standards can specify that debtor countries must be willing to repay debts actively and should be capable of debt management, have sustainable economic and debt plans in place, and guarantee a certain percentage of government revenue or natural resources; and that creditor countries should not interfere in the internal affairs of debtor countries and should take a long view on debt issues. The new mechanism should enable debtor countries to achieve endogenous development of society and economy by tapping the potential of the national economy and strengthening one's own growth drivers after getting financial support; and encourage creditor countries to build a more just and equitable international political and economic order so as to showcase sound effects of the open and shared mechanism for resolving debt defaults.

7.2.4. *Possibilities of entering the Paris Club*

Countries involved in the BRI may consider whether it is possible to join the Paris Club based on their actual overseas investment. First, by joining the club they will gradually make their voice heard in institutional arrangements for global economic governance and further enhance their international influence and credit through cooperation with the Paris Club in specific bailouts. Second, they will get more information on global debtor countries from the Paris Club and reduce the conflicts of interests with related creditor countries. Third, they will slowly increase policy coordination with major creditor countries via the Paris Club, thereby deepening the Western world's understanding of the B&R investment and financing. Last, on the precedent of defending their own political and economic sovereignty, they will seek entry to the Paris Club following the ideas of reform, innovation, win-win and sharing, and on the basis of building a new mechanism for debt restructuring and relief, rather than passively entering the group by yielding to the wills of Western countries.

On the whole, countries involved in the BRI face a dilemma concerning whether to join the Paris Club. However, it is unwise to outrightly say no. There are three options.

Best option: Their entry will be conditional. Existing members of the Paris Club will grant a "transitional period" and "escape clauses" for a period to new members, and will promise they will take the new debt treatment model proposed by new members into full consideration, and work out a substantial "road map" to reform the present debt default-resolving mechanism by factoring in the medium- and long-term sustainable development requirements of debtor countries' economy and society.

Second option: Their entry will be conditional. Existing members of the Paris Club will grant a "transitional period" to new members but hold a neutral attitude (e.g., pending further discussion and negotiation) on whether to reform the existing debt default-resolving mechanism.

So-so option: Their entry will be conditional. But the "transitional period" will be short, with existing members refusing to reform the existing debt default-resolving mechanism and only agree to talk on some technical issues.

However, joining the Paris Club is not a must for countries involved in the BRI. If the conditions for entry are not ripe over a short run, B&R countries can keep the channels of dialogue open or conduct technical discussions with the Paris Club on a country/project basis while protecting their own political and economic sovereignty from being damaged.

8 Stepping up the fight against corruption and commercial bribery in the Belt and Road investment and financing

The fight against corruption and commercial bribery is an important part of international finance. Without a complete set of financial supervisory systems, most countries involved in the Belt and Road Initiative (BRI) face grave challenges and many issues in combating corruption and commercial bribery, and they lack necessary experience in this regard. During investment in and financing for the initiative, it is important to strengthen global cooperation, mobilize all resources, seek proper coordination and carry out well the anti-corruption and commercial bribery measures.

8.1. Corruption and commercial bribery challenges

Corruption undermines economic growth and development, distorts normal market competition, affects the allocation of resources and wastes government funds. An OECD report found that foreign bribes, equaling 10% of the total transaction value and over one-third of the profits on average, pushed up the costs of business operations. Bribes offered by overseas entities also damaged the normal economic order in the market, and resulted in negative relationships between companies and governments because some enterprises illegally secured orders that should have been awarded to others.

According to Transparency International, many countries involved in the BRI do not have comprehensive anti-corruption laws and regulations, and implementation is patchy, which leads to corruption risks in investing and financing activities and project construction. This not only raises the costs of investing in B&R projects but also causes unfair competition. In addition, political rivalries in some of these countries are quite fierce. Corruption can easily become an issue. In countries where there are different attitudes toward China, some people may kick up a controversy over Chinese companies' involvement in bribery cases. This seriously affects bilateral relations, as well as the perception and influence of the Chinese government, companies and financial institutions.

Although tips, agency fees, consulting fees and other kinds of payments are necessary to get business opportunities in many countries and regions involved in the BRI, such monetary benefits may also lead investors to miss competitive opportunities and be punished by law. Corruption is a big concern in B&R investment and financing.

The international community has reached a consensus on strengthening the concerted efforts to combat corruption in international cooperation. President Xi Jinping vowed at the Belt and Road Forum for International Cooperation in 2017 that China would strengthen global anti-corruption cooperation so that the BRI is built on high ethical standards. This requires Chinese companies involved in the BRI to remain clean and say no to corruption and commercial bribery.

8.1.1. *International community combating transnational corruption and commercial bribery across multiple dimensions*

The international community has accumulated lots of experience in guarding against corruption and commercial bribery in global trade, investment and financing.

The Foreign Corrupt Practices Act (the FCPA or the "Act") enacted by the United States in 1977 was the first effort by any nation to specifically criminalize the act of bribing foreign officials. The Lockheed Martin scandal played a pivotal role in the enactment of the FCPA where executives of Lockheed Martin, a large US aerospace and defense company, admitted paying bribes to foreign politicians, including Japan's former Prime Minister Kakuei Tanaka, with the aim of selling Lockheed aircraft. This caused a stir all over the world. The FCPA prohibited US companies from bribing foreign government officials and also defined the compliance management responsibilities of companies. The United States then endeavored to expand the Act's coverage and enhance its international influence. For example, the 1998 amendment further extended the reach to foreign companies and people violating the FCPA within the United States. The Federal Sentencing Guidelines for Organizations (FSGO), issued by the US Sentencing Commission in 1991, explicitly provide that whether a company has established an "effective compliance mechanism" is a key consideration when courts decide how to punish the enterprise.

The Bribery Act, which came into effect in the United Kingdom in 2011, sets forth more stringent requirements on compliance and anti-bribery of companies. Not only does it require companies to operate in compliance, but it also holds them liable for their suppliers, partners, agents and so on. A company without anti-bribery measures can be accused of committing an offense unless it can prove it has "adequate procedures" in place to prevent bribery. Such "adequate procedures" require companies to launch appropriate compliance programs, set up a complete organizational framework for compliance and develop a diverse set of compliance rules.

Sapin II, the French anti-corruption law which came into force in May 2017, tightened the efforts against transnational corruption just like the FCPA and the Bribery Act.

Some countries involved in the BRI have also unveiled relevant laws and regulations, for example, Myanmar's Anti-Corruption Law (2011), Russia's Anti-Corruption Law (2008) and Vietnam's Anti-Corruption Law (2005).

The FCPA, however, put American companies in a disadvantaged position when competing with local companies in countries which did not have such laws and regulations. So the corporate sector in the United States opposed the Act. In response, the US Congress amended the FCPA in 1988 and actively carried out international collaboration to encourage other countries to sign the Act, with the aim of obligating more nations to prevent improper funneling of interests to foreign public officials.

In 1997, OECD accepted the proposal of the United States and issued the Convention on Combating Bribery of Foreign Public Officials in International Business Transactions. The Convention aims to coordinate the efforts of all countries to fight against the bribery of foreign public officials. It contains detailed provisions on conviction of foreign public officials, corporate liability, sanction and jurisdiction, among others, and requires each signatory to perform relevant legislation and law enforcement and provide judicial assistance. So far, 34 OECD member states and seven non-member states, including Russia and Brazil, have signed the Convention, which entered into force in 1999.

As an important international organization to prevent and combat transnational crimes, the United Nations also pays great attention to anti-corruption in international cooperation. The United Nations Convention against Transnational Organized Crime, adopted by the UN General Assembly on November 15, 2000, clearly declares that States Parties shall afford one another the widest measure of mutual legal assistance in investigations, prosecutions and judicial proceedings. In 2005, the United Nations adopted the Convention against Corruption in an effort to curb corruption at its source. The Convention sets forth detailed rules on the conviction of public officials who take bribes, illegally appropriate public property and commit other related offenses, as well as on international cooperation in confiscating and returning proceeds of crime, etc. For example, in terms of preventive anti-corruption policies and practices, the Convention calls on each State Party to establish and promote effective practices aimed at preventing corruption, promote the public's participation and increase transparency; and regarding specific international cooperation, the Convention stipulates that mutual legal assistance shall be afforded to the fullest extent possible with respect to investigations, prosecutions and judicial proceedings, as well as extradition requests, prevention and detection of the transfer of funds of illicit origin, and asset recoveries.

As an influential international organization, the World Bank issued the World Bank Group Integrity Compliance Guidelines, and signed a cross debarment agreement with several other multilateral development banks such as the ADB in 2010. Any company that triggers the cross debarment mechanism will be subject to joint sanctions by these multilateral development banks.

The 2014 Asia-Pacific Economic Cooperation (APEC) Conference in Beijing adopted the Beijing Declaration on Fighting Corruption. China, as the initiator of the Declaration, also participated in the initiation and adoption of the APEC Principles on the Prevention of Bribery and Enforcement of Anti-Bribery Laws and the APEC General Elements of Effective Voluntary Corporate Compliance Programs.

8.1.2. *China to further enhance international cooperation on anti-corruption*

China did not accede to the OECD Convention on Combating Bribery of Foreign Public Officials in International Business Transactions (1997). But it got involved in drafting the United Nations Convention against Corruption, a legal document on worldwide fight against corruption, as soon as the United Nations set up an ad hoc committee in 2000. By virtue of this Convention, which was officially adopted in 2003 and became effective in 2005, China accelerated the cooperation on battling corruption with the rest of the world. In terms of bilateral cooperation, from 2002 to June 2017, the number of countries that have signed extradition treaties with China has increased from 19 to 48, and the number of nations that have signed criminal mutual legal assistance treaties with China has grown from 8 to 59; Chinese procuratorial organs have entered into bilateral cooperation agreements or MOUs with counterparts in more than 90 countries; and China has established international law enforcement cooperation relationships with more than 190 nations. And in terms of multilateral cooperation, to promote the effective implementation of the United Nations Convention against Corruption, the International Association of Anti-Corruption Authorities (IAACA) was established in Beijing in 2006. Through this organization, China has further deepened its global exchanges and cooperation on anti-corruption activity.

Since 2012, the Chinese government has stepped up international cooperation against corruption. The Fourth Plenary Session of the 18th Central Committee of the CPC held in October 2014 wrote, "strengthening international corruption on anti-corruption, doubling the efforts to recover assets and hunt for fugitives, and stepping up repatriation or extradition" into an important document of the Party; on institutional integration, the Central Discipline Inspection Commission adjusted its internal structure and set up the International Cooperation Bureau. Subsequently, the Central Discipline Inspection Commission, the Supreme People's Court, the Supreme People's Procuratorate, the Ministry of Foreign Affairs, the Ministry of Public Security and other three authorities jointly set up the Fugitive Repatriation and Asset Recovery Office of the Central Anti-Corruption Coordination Group that directs the pursuit of assets and fugitives outside China. On international communication mechanisms, the 2014 APEC Conference adopted the Beijing Declaration on Fighting Corruption and proposed to establish the APEC Network of Anti-Corruption Authorities and Law Enforcement Agencies (ACT-NET), marking the entry of anti-corruption efforts in the Asia-Pacific into the substantial cooperation stage from theoretical exchanges. One of the greatest outcomes of the Declaration is the fact that a consensus has been reached on facilitating the sharing of information on international anti-corruption cooperation. The continuous concrete efforts have placed China's international cooperation on combating corruption onto a fast track. On this basis, China captured the opportunity of leading international cooperation on anti-corruption. At the G20 Hangzhou Summit in 2016, G20 leaders endorsed the High Level Principles on Cooperation on Persons Sought for Corruption and Asset Recovery and the 2017–2018 G20 Anti-corruption Action Plan, and decided to establish a research center in China on international cooperation on corruption and asset recovery. All these achievements indicate that China is making new ground in partnering with other countries and regions in the fight against corruption by proposing not only principles but also organizational mechanisms and action plans for international cooperation on anti-corruption.

Some recent cases show that corruption has already become a key risk threatening China's cross-border investment cooperation. According to a study, corruption turned out to be the largest barrier to overseas expansion of Chinese enterprises. The corruption existing in investment and operations has led to loss of state-owned assets, restricted the healthy development and sustainability of profitability of enterprises, and hampered the spread of China's good national image.

Based on the current practices, China needs to double its efforts in countering corruption and commercial bribery abroad. Particularly regarding overseas contracted projects and overseas investment projects, some Chinese enterprises are hiring local "agents" or "brokers" and have to pay them a large commission and consulting and advisory fees. Competent departments should strengthen audit and supervision of these payments. Competent departments should also track and investigate Chinese enterprises or financial institutions suspected of bribery or corruption reported by foreign media.

China has not yet introduced a special law on anti-foreign commercial bribery or anti-foreign corruption, nor has it signed the OECD Convention on Combating Bribery of Foreign Public Officials in International Business Transactions. This shortcoming in both domestic law and international law weighs against China's further work on combating foreign corruption and commercial bribery.

8.1.3. Many causes of corruption in B&R countries

As per the World Bank's report *Doing Business 2017*, countries involved in the BRI vary greatly in business environment. Some of them perform badly and score poorly in such aspects as paying taxes, registering property, dealing with construction permits, accessing credit, resolving insolvency, protecting minority investors and enforcing contracts. The poor business environment often creates inconvenience to Chinese investments, pushes up production and operating costs, raises financial expenses and eats into profits. And enterprises often have to bribe officials to bypass market supervision and related laws and obtain more trading opportunities and benefits.

The phenomenon of the "soft state" is seen in some countries involved in the BRI, where anti-corruption agencies work inefficiently, anti-corruption laws are not strictly implemented and "hidden rules" prevail. This lowers the expectations of foreign investors on clean government and pushes them to achieve business goals through bribery.

Foreign bribery is concentrated in government procurement. As per an OECD study, government-sponsored public procurement reported most foreign bribery cases. In the majority of cases, bribes were paid to obtain public procurement contracts (57%), followed by clearance of customs procedures (12%) and favorable tax treatment (6%). Bribes were promised, offered or given most frequently to employees of public enterprises (state-owned or controlled enterprises) (27%), followed by customs officials (11%), health officials (7%), defense officials (6%), tax officials (4%) and transport officials (3%).

8.2. A multi-pronged approach to push the fight against foreign corruption and commercial bribery

8.2.1. Accelerate legislation of anti-corruption and tighten supervision of overseas investment and operation

A sound law against foreign corruption can prevent enterprises from enduring corruption risks when participating in foreign projects on the institutional sphere. It can urge Chinese enterprises to refuse to bribe foreign public officials and punish those who do not operate in compliance with laws and regulations, thus establishing a clean image for Chinese government and enterprises. Although the Criminal Law of the People's Republic of China, the Anti-unfair Competition Law of the People's Republic of China and the Interim Provisions on Banning Commercial Bribery apply stern sanctions against bribe-taking officials, China has no legal provisions on Chinese enterprises bribing abroad. Thus, it is necessary for China to enact the Law on Anti-foreign Corruption in a bid to safeguard its national image, regulate the acts of Chinese companies abroad and maintain Chinese enterprises' international competitiveness from a long-term perspective.

8.2.2. Government to strengthen guidance, early warning, and supervision, and to blacklist enterprises

The first need is to strengthen publicity and education on investment corruption risks to Chinese enterprises and enable them to firmly establish the awareness of compliant operation. Some enterprises that have gone abroad early and accumulated rich investment experience have begun to attach great importance to overseas investment risk assessment but still do not take corruption risk assessment seriously. In recent years, the payment of huge fines by noncompliant Chinese companies has once again warned other enterprises of the urgency of raising awareness of guarding against overseas investment corruption risks. And the second need is to establish an anti-corruption early warning mechanism and a blacklist system for enterprises engaging in corruption or commercial bribery.

8.2.3. Financial institutions to take effective measures to rein in, prevent and combat corruption and bribery

Anti-corruption and anti-bribery clauses should be added to loan and insurance contracts, making it clear that any bribery by the borrowing company, the insured or a related party will constitute a breach of contract and trigger early repayment, and that the insurer has the right to reject claims. In terms of development aids and officially supported export credits, Chinese financial institutions should take appropriate measures to stop or combat bribery in the business transactions they support with reference to the Recommendation of the OECD Council on Bribery and Officially Supported Export Credits. For example, after approving credit, guarantees and insurance, measures such as refusal to pay, rejection to claims or recovery of already paid money should be taken if bribery is confirmed. In the meantime, financial institutions should co-develop and share the blacklists and build a joint punishment mechanism.

8.2.4. Enterprises to reinforce compliance awareness and improve the capacity for legal compliance and anti-corruption

In the going-global drive, Chinese enterprises should increase awareness of operating business in compliance with laws and regulations, and build and improve their mechanisms for preventing and stopping corruption. They should pay attention to investment strategies instead of looking for instant success and quick profits, prefer business with low corruption risks and strive to eliminate corruption risks. Enterprises should develop a corporate culture of compliant operation, establish the concept of compliant and legal operation and resolutely reject corruption. They should put a transnational compliant operation assessment mechanism in place, set up an internal supervisory body, clearly state the severe punishment mechanism for corruption and reduce the chance of corruption. In the investment risk assessment, enterprises should focus on assessing corruption risks and take targeted measures by type or case of corruption in operations.

8.2.5. Platforms of international organizations to be leveraged in building intergovernmental cooperation and communication mechanisms for anti-commercial corruption

To build a clean Silk Road, China must actively rely on the platforms of different international organizations such as the United Nations, G20, APEC and BRICS, and integrate into the international anti-corruption cooperation network in accordance with the United Nations Convention against Corruption, the OECD Convention on Combating Bribery of Foreign Public Officials in International Business Transactions, the G20 High Level Principles on Cooperation on Persons Sought for Corruption and Asset Recovery and the Beijing Declaration on Fighting Corruption to minimize the possibility of enterprises' overseas corruption. China, which has not signed the OECD Convention on Combating Bribery of Foreign Public Officials in International Business Transactions, needs to earnestly study whether and when to accede to the Convention as Russia, Brazil and Turkey have become signatories. At the same time, China's anti-corruption agencies should ramp up "point-to-point" anti-corruption cooperation with their counterparts in other countries involved in the BRI by signing cooperation agreements; stepping up coordination; unifying standards; building anti-corruption communication, regular consultation and information exchange mechanisms; and institutionalizing the bilateral cooperation on the fight against corporate corruption risks, including investigation and evidence collection, transfer of job-related crime proceedings, extradition and asset recovery and return of bribes. While effectively punishing corruption crimes, China should protect the legitimate rights and interests of Chinese companies and build up its image as a responsible major country.

9 Making the Belt and Road investment and financing information public and transparent

The Belt and Road Initiative is a public good offered by China to the rest of the world. For the initiative to bring common benefits and create common value for countries and international organizations, the key lies in institutional building and providing relevant information to the public in a transparent manner. According to the Chinese government, the BRI is a sunshine initiative and bears the striking characteristics of equality, openness, and inclusiveness. All the participants discuss with each other how to devise the cooperation blueprint and implement specific projects, and everything about the initiative is conducted openly.

9.1. Lack of transparency in the BRI and consequences

Lack of transparency in China's policy announcement, project implementation and other processes, as well as insufficiency of information disclosures, from pre-implementation approval to monitoring during and after project construction, has somewhat damaged the attractiveness and follow-up development of the Belt and Road Initiative.

9.1.1. Opaque supporting policies

As the BRI involves many countries with starkly different national conditions, it is advisable to avoid setting quantified, mandatory investment rules in the specific implementation process but increase flexibility through reducing formal arrangements. However, the bilateral agreements concluded between China and other countries involved in the initiative aimed at strengthening cooperation are generally short of binding force, and can hardly impose effective constraints on host nations. The negotiation process is more complicated because host countries often focus only on their own economic and political interests. Some nations will give up their impractical plans if policies are made more transparent and interest demands of B&R countries are standardized through institutional building. A practical and open institutional platform will help all nations realize wide consultation, joint contribution and shared benefits.

Besides, the international community will challenge the strategic intention of the BRI over lack of transparency in policies. For example, some Westerners argue that China wants to grab market share in other countries via the initiative, control energy and other resources, and manipulate the politics of other nations using debt; and others criticize the poor quality, inefficiency, environment-unfriendliness and corruption of projects under the initiative, and think the BRI is a kind of neocolonialism. China can clear such skepticism and misunderstanding with facts if the Belt and Road-related information is made more public and transparent.

9.1.2. Non-transparent implementation process

9.1.2.1. Transparency of financial plans

The so-called creditor imperialism allegation prevailing in the West claims that China's investment has increased the debt burden of host countries. Although the charge does not bear scrutiny, it shows the importance of enhancing financial transparency of specific projects under the BRI. Countries involved in the BRI are mostly emerging economies with weak solvency. Hence, it is necessary for China to keep in mind financial and fiscal uncertainties when investing in nations along the routes. Transparent investment plans and financial forecasts will counter negative public opinions and speculations in the global community.

9.1.2.2. Competitive bidding

Connectivity of infrastructure and facilities is a key area of the BRI. Competitive bidding is a strict requirement in the international infrastructure sector, and plays a pivotal role in ensuring fair competition, attracting high-quality bidders and guaranteeing the smooth progress of projects. Some Western companies are concerned about unfair competition because they think many projects are funded by Chinese state-owned banks or sovereign wealth funds, and the participants are SOEs. It is true that many projects under the BRI are promoted by the government. Lack of knowledge by the outside world on the projects' early operations and inexactness of the government's public procurement rules will set back cooperation and possibly lead to legal disputes and project delays.

9.1.3. Opaque project information

So far, China has not developed a unified, regular and complete data disclosure platform, blocking the access of other countries and regions to authoritative statistics on the BRI. The Brookings Institution, a US think tank, said in a report that China perplexedly does not disclose loan amounts, terms and names of projects it extends loans to. CDB and Eximbank, which disbursed most of the loans, do not update the loan data (including loan terms), and large Chinese SOEs involved in building roads, railways, ports, power stations and other infrastructure projects often refuse to share data. To get the loan data, researchers have to go to great lengths just to find an estimate. An expert at the Center for Strategic and International Studies in the United States said obtaining the early-stage information, particularly at the tender stage, of projects under the BRI was most difficult. The public does not know when the projects have started, and when they get some information, the projects have already been launched or even completed. Foreign companies may have the chance to join the BRI if they gain access to effective project information at the early stage.

Chinese people and companies have the same urgent demand for authoritative information on the initiative. A questionnaire survey carried out by the Shanghai Academy of Social Sciences in 2017 asked the respondents what kinds of information about the BRI they were most eager to know as the initiative was increasing its international influence. Over 50% of the respondents wanted to know how the initiative would benefit the country; 41.3% wanted to know what major projects have been carried out; and 39.2% were interested in what major plans have been made. The result indicates that the public crave transparent and authoritative information. It is also another way of saying that nontransparent information will possibly become a serious impediment to the attractiveness of the initiative.

9.2. Major experiences of the World Bank on improving investment transparency

The World Bank is the most important international financial institution that lends to developing countries. Since 2008, it has committed itself to improving the openness, transparency and accountability of business and research. This work is backed by, first, the Open Data

Initiative, which provides free and open access to data that was previously restricted to commercial use and was only available to paying users; and second, the World Bank Policy on Access to Information, a landmark disclosure policy that provides the public access to more information than ever before – information about projects under preparation, projects under implementation, analytic and advisory activities, and Board proceedings. Specifically, the "World Bank Maps" and "AidFlows" websites release information about project locations and development assistance in order to improve transparency and strengthen dialogue and citizen participation at the national level. The World Bank Group Finances Initiative makes data related to the group's financials available to everybody in a social, interactive, visually compelling and machine-readable format. It includes the World Bank's commitments and disbursements country by country. Users can segment and visualize data and share the data on their home country's projects online. The Implementation Status and Results (ISR) reports detail the implementation performance and results of World Bank-financed projects, and all ISR reports are published on the World Bank's external website.

In terms of project management, the World Bank has accumulated rich project information from providing financial and technical assistances to creditor countries, and on this basis has developed a complete set of project management framework and models covering feasibility study, design, implementation, monitoring and evaluation. A notable feature is the focus on process monitoring, based on participatory monitoring and evaluation. At the early stage of project design, monitoring indicators suitable for evaluation are designed specific to the characteristics of project construction. This goes side by side with the design of monitoring indicators systems and monitoring manuals, as well as the development of monitoring databases. Using monitoring techniques and methods, stakeholders track and monitor the implementation of projects and provide monitoring analysis results on an annual basis to inform management departments fully of the project progress and relevant issues. Besides, phased supervisory inspections, as well as memos and progress reports, are utilized to further improve the transparency of project implementation.

Consistent with the World Bank's information disclosure policy, the following information is publicly available:

(1) Business information, including more than ten kinds of documents, such as briefings on economic and departmental work, country assistance strategies, project information documents, technical information documents, project evaluation documents, development

policy documents and credit disbursement documents. Under exceptional circumstances, the World Bank may restrict the access to documents which contain significant issues of confidentiality or sensitive information, or whose disclosure could cause harm to specific parties or interests. These documents show "Restricted Information" on the covers.

(2) Research and database information, including economic analyses, research results, external debt data, total estimates of non-guaranteed private debt, short-term loans, future borrowings, and repayment flow data.

(3) Financial information, including financial statements (disclosed on a quarterly basis). Financial statements contain the balance sheet and the income statement, as well as the introduction to relevant financial policies and risk management strategies.

9.3. Strengthening the transparency of B&R investment and financing

We recommend a five-pronged approach for enhancing the transparency of B&R project investment and financing.

9.3.1. Respecting the line

Improving transparency does not mean disclosing all investment and financing information. Market entities, including enterprises and financial institutions, need to join governments in developing unified standards on how to disclose and what kinds of information to reveal. And we must defend the line that the disclosure of information concerning national security, social stability and business secrets is strictly forbidden. Furthermore, with reference to the general practices of the World Bank, AIDB, EDB and other international organizations on credit provisions to projects, China should draft the minimum disclosure standards, outline, framework or catalog for the B&R project investment and financing information. The information disclosure line varies because participants in the initiative include public and private sectors. However, developing and publishing the information disclosure standards will further enhance the transparency of project investment and financing.

9.3.2. Building platforms to publicize and explain the Chinese approach and intention

The international community's skepticism of the B&R information transparency is largely due to misunderstanding, misinterpretation and information asymmetry. Actually, China has published the information on project planning and construction, and other related statistics, to varying degrees on different occasions. But this information is not fully transmitted to stakeholders due to language barriers, cultural differences, decentralization of platforms and lack of publicity. It is advisable to disclose various information from different sources, for example, the National Development and Reform Commission, the Ministry of Foreign Affairs, the Ministry of Finance, financial supervisors and industry associations, across an authoritative, unified and well-known official platform in multiple languages, over different media and in diversified forms. Government and non-government research and exchange platforms, including summits, forms, symposiums and exhibitions, will be leveraged as channels for communication and exchanges. These platforms will present adequate interpretations of the strategic intention and economic and social significance of China's investment in and financing for projects under the BRI in order to minimize negative public opinions and baseless conjectures and provide international investors with transparent information sources.

9.3.3. Urging and overseeing different departments to improve information transparency

Insufficient recognition of the importance of information disclosure, poor implementation and lack of motivation of related departments have resulted in the inadequate disclosure of lots of information that can produce positive social benefits in the BRI. For instance, the information on investment and financing policies, project construction opportunities, project construction statistics, project progress, bidding and tendering information, financing channels and participants can be disclosed properly to meet the requirements of foreign investors. Besides, China should step up the fight against corruption, commercial bribery, fraud and money laundering in the B&R investment and financing by giving full play to the supervisory function of social media, and fully disclosing relevant project information.

9.3.4. Enhancing judicial transparency

China should allow international commercial courts and other legal entities to play their important role in addressing commercial disputes and investor protection cases involved in the B&R project investment and financing, and render effective judicial services and guarantees for the investment in and financing for projects under the BRI. Laws should be enforced strictly, and justice should be impartial to protect the legitimate rights and interests of Chinese and foreign parties on an equal basis and create a stable, fair, transparent and law-based business environment. IT application should be vigorously strengthened at courts, and the results of the "smart court" initiative should be fully leveraged to provide parties with efficient, convenient and intelligent judicial services. China should build and further improve diversified dispute settlement mechanisms that effectively link litigation, mediation and arbitration following the principle of wide consultation, joint contribution and shared benefits. The mechanisms, absorbing and integrating domestic and foreign legal resources, will properly resolve the commercial, trade and investment disputes under the BRI in accordance with the law, so as to remove international investors' doubts about judicial opacity.

9.3.5. Strengthening research to provide theoretical and public opinion support for more transparency

China should give full play to the positive role of financial institutions and think tanks such as universities. Strengthened policy interpretations, in-depth market analyses and special project research will strongly boost the transparency of the BRI. By increasing research and analysis on the potential opportunities, project risks, social benefits and policy difficulties related to the initiative, China will further enhance the transparency of information on its cooperation with other countries involved in the initiative. Studying the debt situation, economic prospects and project construction of relevant nations can provide more valuable information for the decision-making of international investors, reduce information asymmetry and lessen the uncertainties of project investment and financing.

10 Pushing renminbi internationalization to inject new growth momentum into the BRI

Strengthening the financial integration is an important guarantee for the Belt and Road Initiative. And the use of renminbi can effectively reduce exchange costs of other countries involved in the initiative and build up their capacity for countering financial risks. The initiative and the internationalization of renminbi are complementary to each other and mutually reinforcing, with the latter being in a better position to serve the former.

10.1. Use of renminbi in the initiative and obstacles

10.1.1. Analysis

10.1.1.1. BRI fueling renminbi internationalization

10.1.1.1.1. CROSS-BORDER RENMINBI SETTLEMENT

Since the implementation of the Belt and Road Initiative, settlements in renminbi along the B&R countries have surged, and countries and regions engaging in cross-border renminbi receipt and payment business with China have been increasing. As of March 2018, 349,000 companies and over 386 banks in 242 countries and regions conducted cross-border renminbi dealings with China, and banks in 137 countries and regions opened 5,028 accounts with banks in the Chinese mainland.

10.1.1.1.2. RENMINBI CLEARING ARRANGEMENTS

Cross-border renminbi clearing arrangements not only underpin renminbi internationalization but also empower China's financial strength and financial safety. By the end of December 2018, renminbi clearing arrangements had covered 23 countries and regions in Southeast Asia,

Europe, the Americas, Oceania and Africa, including seven B&R countries, namely, Singapore, Qatar, Malaysia, Thailand, Hungary, Russia and the UAE.

For the purpose of further integrating cross-border renminbi clearing channels and offering more efficient settlement services in cross-border renminbi payments, the People's Bank of China has developed renminbi Cross-border Interbank Payment System (CIPS) in phases to pave the way for internationalizing renminbi. The CIPS Phases I and II were launched on October 8, 2015 and May 2, 2018, respectively. As of the end of November 2018, the system had 31 direct participants and 782 indirect ones. As of the end of the third quarter of 2018, the CIPS had processed a total of 1,049,200 transactions involving 19.01 trillion yuan, representing a year-on-year increase of 14.3% and 102.2%, respectively.

10.1.1.1.3. RENMINBI/FOREIGN CURRENCY SWAPS

Since 2008, China has signed bilateral currency swap agreements with a number of countries and regions, aimed at maintaining regional financial stability, promoting bilateral trade and investment facilitation and spurring the internationalization of the renminbi. Over the years, China has conducted currency swap dealings with more nations and regions by gradually expanding the coverage from ASEAN, Japan and South Korea to Central Asia, South Asia, Europe and Latin America. Countries and regions involved in the BRI are the main parties of currency swaps. By December 2018, China's central bank had entered into bilateral currency swap agreements valued at 3.3 trillion yuan with central banks and monetary authorities of 37 countries and regions, including 22 countries along the Belt and Road, and the bilateral currency swap agreements signed with Hungary, Albania, Europe, Switzerland, Sri Lanka, Russia, Qatar, Iceland and Indonesia exceeded 1.4 trillion yuan in value.

10.1.1.1.4. DIRECT RENMINBI TRADING

In order to promote bilateral trade and investment, the People's Bank of China has taken steps to galvanize the direct trading of renminbi with foreign currencies since 2012. The country's interbank foreign exchange market already hosts direct trading of a number of currencies, including the Japanese yen, Australian dollar and British pound. Currencies of B&R countries in direct trading with renminbi include the UAE dirham, Saudi riyal, Hungarian forint, Polish zloty, Turkish lira and Thai baht. The brisk direct renminbi trading in the interbank foreign exchange market has significantly improved liquidity and saved exchange costs for micro-economic entities.

10.1.1.2. *Existing issues*

The countries involved in the Belt and Road Initiative are not issuers of the most popular currencies. Therefore, their trading, investing and financing activities are overwhelmingly dominated by the third-party currencies, typically the US dollar. Although China has become the world's second-largest economy and the largest trading nation, the country's main trade partners are still the United States and European countries using the dollar or the euro as the quotation and settlement currency, which greatly restricts the renminbi's pricing function. China imports a large quantity of intermediate products from Japan, Brazil, Australia, South Korea and Taiwan Province, processes and assembles them into finished products in the mainland, and finally exports the finished products mainly to developed nations such as the United States and the EU. At the same time, China imports energy, oil and other resources in bulk, and these resources are mostly priced in US dollars in the international market. Overall, the use of renminbi in B&R countries and regions is lower than expected.

With regard to cross-border settlements, actual cross-border renminbi receipts and payments between China and other countries involved in the BRI reached 778.6 billion yuan in 2016, accounting for 7.9% of the total during the period. One year later, the amount and share had risen to over 1.36 trillion yuan and 14.7%, respectively. The past two years show that the percentage of cross-border transactions settled in renminbi along the B&R was lower than 25% overall. Specifically, the percentage surpassed 10% in seven countries only, stood at 5–10% in two countries and was below 5% in the remaining 55 countries. We can see from the distribution of renminbi use that the currency is mainly used in several core areas such as Singapore, Malaysia and Vietnam. Regarding currency swaps, although China has signed 1.4 trillion-yuan worth of currency swap agreements with other countries involved in the BRI, the effective amount stands at about 20–30 billion yuan only. From the angle of direct currency transactions, the financial institutions of B&R nations are willing to participate in direct trading, but they require local branches of Chinese banks and third-party financial institutions to work together because their countries have small currency transactions but big currency movements. What's more, the direct trading between the renminbi and currencies of other countries in the initiative has to go through complex procedures.

These stumbling blocks make it difficult for B&R countries to obtain renminbi.

10.1.2. Capital account and financial supervisory policies restricting investment and financing

Over the past several years, Chinese and foreign financial markets have witnessed continuing big fluctuations due to changes in the economic environment at home and abroad. This has led to some important adjustments in China's financial supervisory policies on cross-border capital flows. In spite of no nominal restrictions, there are actually rigorous, prudent supervisory measures in place, affecting investing and financing activities under the BRI.

10.1.2.1. Foreign exchange administration policies are behind the curve

Overseas business accounts of Chinese enterprises are governed by the Regulations on Administration of Overseas Foreign Exchange Accounts (No. 10 document of the State Administration of Foreign Exchange in 1997). The situation at home and abroad has changed a lot compared with when the Regulations was released, making it difficult for companies to perform overseas account management as per the Regulations. Besides, there is a lack of transparency in foreign exchange administration policies. The supervisory authority advises banks via so-called window guidance, but banks have different understandings of window guidance. As a result, some banks can handle the business, but others cannot, and even different branches of a bank may apply different handling standards. This adds difficulties to overseas business growth and negotiations of enterprises.

10.1.2.2. Cross-border capital flows are subject to strict reviews and restrictions

In recent years, the Chinese government has tightened capital flows across borders. Iron-handed control over the expatriation of domestic capital has been conducive to maintaining the stability of renminbi exchange rates and protecting the safety of China's foreign exchange reserves. But the exhaustive foreign exchange review procedures have hampered the functioning of companies' cross-border fund pools, and the money needed by some projects cannot be transferred abroad in time, raising corporate costs.

10.1.2.3. Registration and filing of offshore bond issuing is cumbersome and inflexible

According to the Notice on Promoting the Administrative Reform of the Filing and Registration System for Issuance of Foreign Bonds by Enterprises issued by the National Development and Reform Commission in 2015, the previous approval system implemented for issuance of foreign bonds has been replaced by a filing and registration system. However, companies still have to go through cumbersome filing procedures with the competent department for issuing foreign debts. There is a high demand on time windows and lack of flexibility. In addition, without an effective interdepartmental coordination mechanism in place, related departments are not coordinated enough in supervising enterprises' overseas investment, while bond issuing review and approval is still overseen by multiple supervisory agencies, causing inconvenience to corporate investment and financing abroad.

10.1.2.4. Strict constraints on the use of financial derivatives in overseas investment and financing

In the BRI-related investing and financing activities, enterprises are exposed to big market risks, including fluctuations in interest rates, exchange rates and commodity prices in the host countries. They are required to actively use interest rate, exchange rate and other derivatives; strengthen cooperation with financial institutions; work out reasonable hedging programs; and reduce market risks. However, in actual practice, relevant state-owned assets supervisors are very prudent and have imposed strict assessment requirements on enterprises. It is thus difficult for many companies to flexibly use derivatives to hedge market risks.

10.1.2.5. Some investment restricted by the industry guidance policy on foreign direct investment

In recent years, national authorities have addressed investments of some companies such as asset transfers via outbound investment. According to the Notice on Forwarding the Guiding Opinions on Further Directing and Regulating the Direction of Overseas Investments released in 2017, real estate, cinemas and sports clubs fall into the category of restricted overseas investments, while companies' large value and irrational investments in their non-principal sectors shall be reviewed strictly. Actually, these measures will also affect normal overseas investments of enterprises. In particular, discretion is often exercised over whether an investment along the Belt and Road is rational or not, somewhat restricting investment and financing.

10.2.   Improving financial markets and supervision, and connecting Chinese and foreign financial markets

10.2.1.   *Ameliorating quotation and settlement of commodities in renminbi*

Among countries involved in the BRI, the Middle Eastern nations, Russia and Central Asian countries are exporters of resources such as crude oil and natural gas, while major emerging economies such as China, India and ASEAN member states are important importers. Based on the most basic economic principle that supply and demand determines price in a market, B&R countries should be major determinants of the prices of commodities such as crude oil and natural gas. However, since financial derivatives with energy products as the underlying assets are quite developed, the spot price of energy products is hardly determined by market supply and demand but is mainly linked to futures prices. The major crude oil futures markets are located in the United States and developed European nations, and they are dominated by major international financial institutions. What's more, the value of the US dollar and the monetary policy of the Federal Reserve can also significantly influence crude oil and its financial derivatives which are denominated in the US dollar, thereby further magnifying the flaws of the international monetary system. Similarly, in the gold market the gold price is mainly determined by participants in the London and New York markets.

The crude oil futures market and the gold market (spot and futures) are important components of the international financial market. Whether the renminbi can play a role in pricing in these two markets matters to the internationalization of the currency. In September 2014, the International Board of Shanghai Gold Exchange was officially launched in the China (Shanghai) Pilot Free Trade Zone. In July 2015, Shanghai-Hong Kong Gold Connect was rolled out to connect the mainland's and Hong Kong's gold markets. In April 2016, the Shanghai Gold Exchange published the world's first renminbi-denominated Shanghai Gold Benchmark Price, a move set to shake up the global gold market currently dominated by US dollar trading in London and New York. On March 26, 2018, renminbi-denominated crude oil futures contracts were put on trading at the Shanghai International Energy Exchange. This was followed by the delivery of crude oil futures contract SC1809, the first main contract, on September 7, 2018. The smooth completion of the first delivery marks a milestone, shows the recognition of China's crude oil futures by businesses in real economy and will attract many other businesses to participate in and use the crude oil futures market. In the near term, it is difficult for renminbi-denominated Shanghai crude oil futures to challenge or supersede the US dollar-denominated oil products. But in the longer-term horizon, the denomination of oil in multi-currencies will define the future, in which the renminbi is set to play a part.

To improve the renminbi pricing service for commodities, China may prioritize the following tasks. The first task is to speed up the optimization of the "Shanghai Gold" pricing mechanism and explore renminbi pricing mechanisms for other precious metals such as silver, platinum and palladium. By introducing more international financial institutions, diversifying the product mix in trading and relaxing trading restrictions, China can facilitate trading and tap the potential of settling commodity and futures transactions in renminbi for better "futures-spots cooperation". The second task is to optimize the participants in the renminbi-denominated commodities market and the participant structure. China may build account systems suitable for commodity trading by country, and encourage key upstream and downstream enterprises in the industrial chain to enter the futures market. The country may engage more foreign traders (e.g., multinationals, internationally important crude oil traders and investment banks) into the market. The third task is to perfect the renminbi trading mechanism for commodities. Exchange rate risk management instruments and supply chain trade finance solutions can be utilized to reasonably reduce investors' operating risks and costs, and improve trading activity and level. And the fourth task is to improve the renminbi foreign exchange market. In the long run, as foreign investors gain bigger exposure to the Chinese currency, foreign exchange hedging will be in enormous demand. Fluctuations in the renminbi exchange rate, hedging convenience and costs will weigh on investment decisions or asset allocations. The foreign exchange market will be increasingly essential to overall allocations.

10.2.2. *Further opening up capital markets*

China's capital markets are opening at a faster pace; especially the interbank bond market is almost fully liberalized, providing huge investment opportunities for other countries involved in the BRI and laying a foundation for deeper renminbi internationalization.

10.2.2.1.   Building an international panda bond market

Panda bond is an important way of financing the BRI and a key carrier of renminbi internationalization. Since September 2015, panda bonds have been issued much more frequently. The main issuers include foreign non-financial enterprises, financial institutions, international development institutions and foreign governments. In 2018, the Shanghai Stock Exchange and the Shenzhen Stock Exchange issued the requirements for improving the panda bond financing mechanism for the BRI, supporting relevant institutions, high-quality enterprises and international financial institutions of China and other countries in the initiative, to issue renminbi bonds in China. On September 25, 2018, the People's Bank of China and the Ministry of Finance jointly issued the Interim Measures for the Administration of Bond Issuance by Overseas Institutions in the National Interbank Bond Market, the first systematic regulation to govern the panda bond market. It is expected that this preferential regulation will drive China's panda bond market to even bigger success. In the future, China should encourage governments, financial institutions or enterprises of more countries involved in the BRI to finance projects under the BRI by offering panda bonds.

10.2.2.2.   Continuing to expand the connectivity of capital markets

In the stock market, the "Shanghai-London Stock Connect" program, another endeavor after the "Shanghai-Hong Kong Stock Connect" and "Shenzhen-Hong Kong Stock Connect" programs, achieved fast progress in 2018. Shanghai-London Stock Connect brings together the Shanghai Stock Exchange and the London Stock Exchange, and is expected to enhance the function of the renminbi in international financial transactions at three levels. The first level involves expanding the product category and coverage for renminbi asset allocations, and boosting the attractiveness of renminbi assets via the Chinese and British stock markets. China's stock markets are becoming more attractive to global investors with the second-largest market capitalization in the world, and the inclusion of Shanghai and Shenzhen listed stocks into the MSCI Emerging Markets Index in 2018. The United Kingdom owns the largest stock market in Europe, while the London Stock Exchange underwrites over two-thirds of the world's stocks, attracting global capital which can provide vast space for renminbi allocations and uses. The second level involves driving the advancement of China's capital markets and supporting the internationalization of the renminbi. Presently, China's capital markets are still in the early days of internationalization. Shanghai-London Stock Connect is conducive to spurring the connectivity of domestic and foreign capital markets; bringing freshness into related rules and regulations, philosophies and behavioral patterns; ameliorating the structure of participants; scaling up transactions; propelling appropriate competition; increasing the maturity and international influence of China's capital markets; and bolstering the internationalization of the renminbi. The third level involves joining the two international financial centers – London and Shanghai – in providing a broad platform for renminbi uses. Based on Shanghai-London Stock Connect, the two cities will work together and complement each other for common development, in an effort to back the circulation of and trading in renminbi across borders.

In the bond market, "Bond Connect", which premiered on July 3, 2017, has reported a steadily growing participation and continuously improving transactions. As of the end of June 2018, 356 foreign institutional investors from 21 countries and regions entered the interbank bond market through the "Bond Connect" program. It is expected that Bond Connect will be extended to include Southbound Trading at a later stage. This is important to further open the domestic bond market and establish a system of renminbi circulation on and outside the Chinese mainland. For this reason, China should accelerate the start of Southbound Trading under Bond Connect, continuously expand the bi-directional openness of finance, and thus lay a good institutional foundation for renminbi internationalization.

10.2.3. *Offering more offshore renminbi financial products*

The expansion of cross-border renminbi business scope and the steady progress in renminbi internationalization are accompanied by the rapid growth of offshore renminbi (CNH) business. Hong Kong, Singapore, Taiwan, London and Luxembourg have become main CNH markets.

In recent years, CNH business volume and product types have increased significantly. Take Hong Kong as an example. At present, the main renminbi business there includes CNH deposits, investment deposits (currency-linked deposits) and dim sum bonds. In the offshore derivatives market, USD/CNH futures is a main product of CNH futures, and accounted for 98.5% of all CNH futures at the end of 2017. In addition, USD/CNH options, EUR/CNH futures, JPY/CNH futures and AUD/CNH futures have been rolled out one after another.

At the same time, London's CNH market has quickly grown from nothing to the largest CNH center in the West and the second-largest in the world. In particular, since the foreign exchange reform in 2015, the CNH market in London has stood out with extraordinary performance, becoming the world's largest CNH foreign exchange trading center and the second-largest center of payment and clearing in CNH. According to SWIFT, in March 2018, renminbi foreign exchange transactions in the United Kingdom had a 38.63% share of the world's total, much higher than the Hong Kong market (26.65%). In April 2018, transactions paid in renminbi in the United Kingdom represented 5.97% of the global total, second only to Hong Kong.

Looking ahead, the general trend of renminbi internationalization will guide CNH business onto a broader arena. In addition to focusing services on providing basic financial products such as cross-border clearing and settlement in renminbi, renminbi deposit and loan and unsecured guarantee in renminbi, the CNH financial markets led by that in Hong Kong can also offer green renminbi bonds, renminbi-denominated asset-backed securities (ABS) products and renminbi reinsurance products, among others; optimize renminbi cash and risk management services; and help widen the use of renminbi while promoting multiple functions such as cross-border renminbi financing/settlement.

In terms of the layout of CNH centers, China should not only develop the CNH centers in Hong Kong, London and so on but also respond to demands of other places by tailor-making renminbi products based on local advantages and gradually extending the reach to such places. That is, a CNH market system based in Hong Kong and with presence in other financial centers will be built to drive the internationalization of renminbi. When the renminbi becomes freely convertible, overseas renminbi financial assets can be allocated on the basis of market demand and all CNH centers should be encouraged to compete and cooperate. In the meantime, China should speed up the development of the Shanghai financial center and ensure that markets at home and abroad are connected effectively.

10.2.4. Setting up a trading center of investment and financing products

The BRI has sizeable and complicated financial needs. The varied development state of financial markets in countries involved in the initiative makes it difficult to unify the pricing, issuing and risk management models and to lower investment and financing costs. Therefore, it becomes particularly important to establish a unified financial product trading platform, for which Shanghai, as the most crucial renminbi financial center, boasts natural advantages. The city is actively pushing bi-directional opening and connectivity of financial markets, attracting financial institutions to play an active part in the BRI and strengthen financial ties with countries and regions along the routes. In the next step, Shanghai will become the B&R investment and financing center and global renminbi financial services center by pursuing financial reform and innovation of its free trade zone and catering much better to the financial service needs of countries and regions involved in the initiative.

Banks should actively explore the B&R project development and cultivation model and mechanism, and support Shanghai to build a pool of major B&R projects. China may create a sharing and joint management model of risks across different regions, put in place a market-oriented global risk management platform, strengthen the innovation of risk management tools and encourage all parties to participate in global risk management of B&R projects.

China should speed up the innovation of renminbi financial products; diversify financial derivatives such as renminbi interest rate swaps, futures and options; increase the stock of CNH capital; and broaden the channels of renminbi capital inflows. Efforts should also be made to accelerate the development of the international renminbi credit market; ramp up international cooperation of bond markets; increase short-term bonds in issuance to boost the short-term government bond market; develop ABS, panda bonds and Mulan bonds; and enhance the participation of domestic and overseas institutions. Cross-border market linkage with international trading platforms and central securities depositories should be improved in terms of business, mechanisms and institutional arrangements.

10.3. Improving the renminbi internationalization policy system

10.3.1. *Allowing better coordination between macro policies and supervision*

As the Chinese economy is expanding its international influence, the country's monetary policies are augmenting spillover effects on the BRI. As a major responsible country, China should fully assess the effects of monetary policies to be developed and any proposed adjustments to monetary policies on the B&R investing and financing activities and on financial asset prices and solvencies of related countries. Therefore, it is important to promote monetary policy cooperation and coordination, and improve the supervision transparency of enterprises and financial institutions and unity of related supervision standards. In a changeable policy environment, China should step up the guidance on overseas risk management to enterprises and financial institutions and improve their capacity for countering risks. The country may unveil guidelines on how companies manage overseas risks; incorporate risk management and control, cost control, uncertainty reduction and other philosophies into corporate rules and regulations; and urge enterprises and financial institutions to reinforce management and control risks. The risk limits companies can tolerate in overseas risk management should be made clearer, with autonomy granted to them within such limits. China should relax the restrictions on enterprises' derivative trading, reduce approval procedures and guide enterprises to respond actively and flexibly to market risks through a reasonable use of derivatives. The country should also perfect the incentive and restraint mechanism in respect of enterprises' management of relevant risks and fully mobilize their enthusiasm and activeness in business expansion and risk management.

10.3.2. Advancing capital account convertibility

China should pursue steady advances in capital account convertibility consistent with the two fundamental principles – furthering reform and opening up, and preventing risks. To this end, it is necessary to make supervision more efficient and effective, and guard against cross-border capital flow risks. To better support genuine and compliant foreign trade and investment, and further improve the management of overseas lending under domestic guarantee, China should develop special measures for supporting the BRI on the basis of avoiding flaws by (1) simplifying the approval process of overseas lending under domestic guarantee, granting qualified enterprises quotas of overseas lending under domestic guarantee and allowing them to provide external guarantees within the quotas after filing; and (2) easing controls or restrictions on capital refluxes of overseas lending under domestic guarantee and permitting foreign debtors to transfer guaranteed money, directly or indirectly, back to the mainland in forms of domestic lending or equity investment.

China should actively tap new areas and new methods concerning how foreign exchange administration of capital items can better serve the real economy, push ahead with stable reforms in foreign exchange administration of cross-border securities investment and expand the bi-directional opening of financial markets. Cross-border capital flow risks should be earnestly forestalled by further improving the foreign debt and capital flow management systems under the macro-prudential policy framework and continuing to consolidate counting and monitoring, as well as interim and ex-post supervision of capital items. China should provide certain preferential policies and flexible arrangements for enterprises' investment in and financing for the BRI; extend further support to foreign exchange purchases with a real business background, genuine exchange purchasing need and contract provisions; and prevent default risks from exchanges. The country should also avoid changing foreign exchange policies frequently so as to stabilize the expectations of enterprises on foreign business and reduce the losses from policy uncertainty. China should update foreign exchange administration regulations in a timely manner in alignment with economic conditions at home and abroad, simplify the procedures of receiving and paying foreign exchanges and facilitate enterprises to schedule when to pay.

The system of bond issuing by companies outside the mainland should be improved through simplifying bond issuing procedures where appropriate and providing more flexible policies for those with real overseas financing demands. For instance, a company can file the annual total bond issuing amount and decide at its discretion how much is to be issued each time in light of actual conditions, that is, issuing first and then registration.

10.3.3. Empowering central banks' currency swap agreements to play a bigger and more effective role

The economies of countries involved in the BRI are vulnerable to external shocks. So they are strongly motivated to pursue monetary cooperation. A good monetary cooperation mechanism will not only help deepen China's financial cooperation with other countries and promote trade and investment but also facilitate the strengthening of a financial safety net over B&R countries and improve their ability to cope with financial crises.

Currently, there is already a foundation for using the renminbi to settle trade and conduct financial investment, but it has not yet become a true "anchor currency" in the region. Therefore, regional monetary and financial cooperation needs to be reinforced. China should make active efforts to institutionalize the Chiang Mai Agreement, while B&R countries should improve regional economic monitoring and policy dialogue mechanisms, and establish a regional monetary fund consisting of their home currencies. At the same time, China should move more quickly to shore up the weak areas in regional financial markets and infrastructure construction, accelerate the development of regional capital markets, cement the role of the renminbi in regional bond markets, design a plan for joint issuance of regional bonds and a plan for placement of corporate bonds, establish a regional credit rating agency and help the renminbi become a major currency for financial investment and trading in the region.

China should continue to expand the volume of bilateral currency swaps and focus on promoting the signing of currency swap agreements with B&R countries. In addition to providing liquidity support during a crisis, the currency swap agreements signed by the People's Bank of China are more significant in driving bilateral trade and investment. If an enterprise of the foreign side to the agreement needs renminbi, it can apply to a commercial bank of its country, which then applies to the central bank, and the central bank exchanges home currency to renminbi with China's central bank. The central bank provides renminbi financing to the commercial bank and eventually the domestic enterprise after getting renminbi to support the import of goods from the Chinese mainland. Similarly, the country or region can also directly collect renminbi for exports to China. This kind of currency swap arrangements can effectively avoid exchange rate risks, reduce exchange costs and fuel bilateral and multilateral trade. Besides, in the event of a liquidity squeeze, support can be provided through bilateral currency swap agreements.

10.3.4. Exploring the setup of overseas capital trading and settlement centers for central enterprises

China's large central enterprises have put in place a fund pool management system in order to maximize fund use efficiency and reduce financial costs. However, the government's increased intervention in and regulation over cross-border capital flows since the exchange reform in 2015 have posed barriers to companies' use of the fund pool channel, and the capital required by some projects could not be transferred outside, impairing the facilitation of renminbi flows across borders. A group of Chinese central enterprises have tried in different ways to effectively address capital controls of China or host countries. For example, Zimbabwe has been facing a shortage of US dollars in recent years. A Chinese company signed a dollar swap agreement with a local Chinese company because the latter had a large amount of dollars and could give dollars to the former in Zimbabwe while the former repaid the latter in renminbi in China. This solved the US dollar financing difficulty of the former in Zimbabwe and reduced dollar flows from China.

In the future, Chinese banks may set up overseas capital trading and settlement centers at the whole-enterprise level in some countries with foreign exchange controls and relative concentration of "going-global" Chinese companies to coordinate central enterprises' currency swaps and match companies with foreign exchange income directly with those with foreign exchange demand to reduce exchange risks.

10.3.5. Encouraging enterprises and financial institutions to use hedging instruments reasonably

While trading in financial derivatives, companies should aim at mitigating risks and locking in costs and rein in arbitrages and speculative transactions.

First, China should urge companies to develop a full set of financial derivative trading management measures. It should be made clear that financial derivative business must be based on genuine orders or trade contracts and aimed at preserving value, while the product in trading, as well as the volume, direction and tenor of trading, should suit the characteristics of hedge trading. Speculation should be strictly prohibited. Companies should recognize the financial and labor costs of hedging, differentiate hedging and speculation, and on this basis develop hedging performance evaluation methods. Before making the decision on investing abroad, companies should take possible conversion risks into full account, validate or assess hedging costs independently in investment return calculation models.

Second, the companies should choose proper financial derivative trading business. Following the principles of simplicity, feasibility and risk controllability, companies should mainly select financial derivatives with simple structures, strong liquidity and controllable risks, and avoid complex business whose risks and pricing are difficult to recognize or evaluate, financial derivative business that does not match one's own business, or medium- and long-term financial derivative business. If the duration of underlying assets (or liabilities) covers the full economic cycle, companies should hedge mainly in a natural way and not engage in derivative trading.

Third, information exchanges and hedging cooperation with financial institutions should be strengthened. Enterprises should be encouraged to regularly exchange information with financial institutions and keep abreast of the latest developments in the international market. And they should adjust hedging strategies in a timely manner and lock in relevant risks in advance, capitalizing fully on the experiences and advantages of financial institutions in managing risks such as interest rate and exchange rate risks.

10.3.6. *Stepping up cooperation of ECAs and coordination in export credit policies*

China should bring the supportive role of export credit to investment and financing under the BRI into full play and attract more capital and market entities in the region to join the initiative. A Chinese agency may take the lead in organizing counterparts in other B&R countries to carry out policy research and coordination, and setting up a platform for peers to consult, discuss and exchange. They may tap business cooperation in credit grants, insurance and reinsurance, to name just a few, on the basis of policy coordination, and back more market entities within or outside the region to invest in or finance the initiative.

Overriding consideration may be given to collaboration on overseas guarantees. In cross-border investment and financing, if the guarantor or collateral is located abroad, it is important to check carefully local legal requirements on guarantor and collateral, e.g., whether there is the required qualification and capacity for providing guarantee and the performance ability. What's more, extra attention should be given to restrictions on provision of guarantee by guarantor or mortgaging of some assets if any in local laws, e.g., the requirements on registration, pre-registration approval, transfer and cashing. Countries involved in the BRI may conclude a legally binding agreement and enter into a regional cooperative relationship concerning collateral registration and query, enforcement of court decisions, collateral disposal and so on, in a bid to create a better investment and financing environment.

11 Improving other areas of the soft environment

Other aspects in relation to the B&R investment and financing, including corporate social responsibility, cross-border taxation, financial innovation, intermediary service, and alignment of technical standards, also need continuous improvement.

11.1. Implementing environmental, labor and corporate social responsibilities

Countries involved in the Belt and Road Initiative have a common goal and responsibility – protecting the environment and increasing employment. Performing social responsibilities can generate long-term benefits for companies, and it is a natural element of building a community with a shared future for mankind. China should well publicize and act on the "green" and "eco-environmental protection" concepts; urge all relevant parties to enhance policy coordination and global cooperation on environmental protection, labor rights, social responsibilities and so on, by building consensus; guide market entities to increase inputs in environmental and labor protection; and monitor whether they are compliant in those endeavors, in a bid to realize a green BRI. China should also bolster the support for green investment and financing, develop green finance, add environmental, labor and corporate social responsibility clauses into investment and financing agreements, and convince more people to show recognition of projects under the BRI for closer people-to-people exchanges.

11.1.1. Enhancing coordination on environmental protection

11.1.1.1. Strengthen research on environmental laws

China should become familiar with other countries' environmental laws and standards, and display environmental consciousness at the time of signing project contracts. To boost research on environment laws of other nations involved in the BRI, first, China should learn good practices from them, and second, it should provide funding and technical assistance to their environmental lawmaking and environmental industry and help countries lagging behind in environmental protection develop environmental laws and regulations, and relevant sectors by offering targeted advice, thus laying a sound foundation for investing in and financing B&R projects there.

11.1.1.2. Reinforce interactions with international organizations to share workload and responsibility

For smooth progress under the BRI, China should engage international organizations to jointly perform and share environmental responsibilities. Drawing on the practice of the World Bank and ADB that requires invested projects to be environment friendly, China should also raise environmental requirements on specific assistance programs, but it should never interfere in host countries' environmental sovereignty while pursuing cooperation on projects under the BRI. For years, the World Bank has been requiring financed projects to make environmental promises, or else it will not invest.

11.1.1.3. Join hands with NGOs in protecting the environment

Some Chinese projects in Africa are opposed by local nongovernmental organizations (NGOs) as they are concerned that Chinese companies are shifting excess capacity and pollution to other countries. So, these projects have suffered a setback. China's investment in Myanmar to build dams and oil and gas pipelines has a large environmental impact. Even if it invests heavily in environmental protection and has support from the local government, the project will face opposition from NGOs and ordinary people. In short, joining hands with the local people and NGOs has a direct influence on the implementation of cooperative projects. Therefore, China should select and support impartial nongovernmental environmental organizations to actively carry out people-to-people exchanges abroad. There are a large number of nongovernmental environmental organizations in China, and they have played a significant role in the country's environmental protection. China should value the role they play in the implementation of the BRI. Chinese investors and companies planning to invest abroad should select and support unbiased nongovernmental environmental organizations to join hands and strengthen people-to-people contacts in the project countries and regions.

11.1.1.4. Build and improve the environmental management system of going-global enterprises

Environmental standards and responsibilities should be made a basic condition for initiating B&R investment and financing projects. And the one-vote veto system should apply to any investment projects that do not meet the environmental standards. The implementation of projects under the BRI should conform to uniform norms and standards, and also learn from international conventions on energy conservation and emissions reduction, so that the entire process from project planning and design to launch and construction complies with environmental standards. China should put domestic enterprises investing abroad under a supervision system, an environmental credit evaluation mechanism and a blacklist system, and build an evaluation system for the green investment of large enterprises. The environmental protection information of projects should be made open and transparent, while environmentally unqualified enterprises should be banned from going global. Moreover, follow-up environmental inspection of completed projects should be conducted as well. All enterprises and personnel should receive environmental protection training before going to the project site.

11.1.1.5. Establish and improve the green financial system

All market entities that invest and finance, especially financial institutions, should play a vital role in building a green "Belt and Road". Multilateral institutions, such as the World Bank, ADB and AIIB, have always emphasized the importance of environmental protection in international investing and financing activities. The World Bank has long incorporated environmental considerations into lending, investment and risk assessment procedures. International experience proves that more and more national governments and international organizations tend to use economic leverage to guide environmental protection.

Although Chinese financial institutions that play a primary role in the B&R investment and financing, such as CDB, Eximbank and the Silk Road Fund, place a high premium on the environmental issue in investment and financing, they still fall short of meeting the World

Bank standards. It deserves careful study on how to develop a complete suite of scientific and reasonable environmental policies for investment and financing based on the actual development of countries involved in the initiative and the development needs of their people. On the one hand, high standards will not be conducive to promoting projects and launching financing, but on the other, low standards will easily result in limited capital going into polluting projects and trigger the international community's distrust or misunderstanding of China's responsibility toward the environment.

11.1.2. *Improving labor cooperation mechanisms and policies for closer people-to-people ties*

Chinese enterprises must strictly abide by the requirements of local immigration bureaus on work visas, and should not do business with low-priced but unqualified agencies and send workers abroad on business or education visas. Moreover, Chinese expatriates should always carry relevant personal documents, and understand and cooperate with local authorities. When hiring local workers, Chinese companies should carefully calculate payroll and training costs, with particular emphasis on their capabilities and experience, and attach importance to the management of local workers. It is necessary to strengthen the training of local employees, enhance their capabilities through training and help them command technology so that they will appreciate and thank Chinese employers from the bottom of their hearts.

While protecting their own legitimate rights and interests, Chinese enterprises should focus on improving the quality and structure of Chinese employees working abroad by moderately reducing the percentage of low-skilled laborers and increasing skilled and technical workers. Chinese enterprises should strengthen the training of exported workers and work earnestly to improve the quality of dispatched persons. In addition, Chinese companies should properly handle various relationships with the locals. They should tailor-make factory establishment plans in local areas based on ground conditions, hire locals to participate in management and production, know how to allow locals to manage their compatriots well and actively create job opportunities for neighborhoods. Furthermore, Chinese companies must respect local religious practices, carry out activities in accordance with local customs, actively fulfill social responsibilities, donate money to assist the local poor and help locals build roads, hospitals, schools and other facilities.

11.2. Bolstering intermediary service mechanism

The B&R investment and financing intermediary services, still in their infancy, can hardly meet the needs of project investment and financing in many aspects. Countries involved in the BRI should quicken the development of related intermediary agencies; improve their professionalism in providing legal, credit rating and information services and so on; and pay due attention to the building of specialized B&R credit rating agencies and an intermediary service database.

11.2.1. Making financial management services more efficient

First, China should motivate other countries involved in the BRI to abide by international accounting standards; implement uniform accounting standards; strengthen talks on accounting, auditing, tax management and so on; and create good institutional conditions and external environment for accounting firms and other intermediary service providers to play a bigger role.

Second, China should strengthen accounting and auditing infrastructure, make financial management and calculations scientific and reliable, and increase Internet technology support for accounting services of relatively underdeveloped B&R nations through assistance and other methods.

Third, intermediary agencies related to financial management in B&R countries should adapt to changes in the international trading environment, continuously improve their ability to interpret different supervisory policies and provide more types of commercial audit services, especially the audits spanning the entire process of corporate investment and the whole process of project investment and financing, and covering all companies and financial institutions involved in the capital flows, so as to help resolve the complex trade and investment issues in the BRI.

Last, multi-talented financial management specialists, professional teams and specialized agencies that look at everything from an international perspective, agree with the B&R development philosophies and are familiar with the history and culture of different countries should increase exchanges and communication. If necessary, countries with relatively advanced financial management services can establish long-term training mechanisms for financial management workers in relatively underdeveloped nations, and thus gain access to their accounting service market.

11.2.2. Balancing the development of credit rating agencies

First, an independent credit rating agency in which China will lead other countries involved in the BRI should be established as soon as possible on the basis of integrating existing rating agencies in B&R countries and their main credit rating research findings. The agency will release different credit ratings based on evaluation of country, investment, buyer, bank, exchange and bond risks in connection with the BRI. It should be an independent, market-oriented entity with commercialized operations under proper policy support from national governments. China must play a leading role in the process of establishing the agency by integrating the researchers and research resources of existing research institutes, policy-oriented financial institutions and commercialized consulting and rating companies, and selecting a socially influential agency with strong research power to render credit rating services for the initiative. SINOSURE has released country risk ratings for 14 years in a row since 2005 and sovereign credit risk ratings for three consecutive years since 2016. The rating results are being recognized by the credit rating industry and academic community, and have produced good social effects. The Chinese government can permit SINOSURE, a policy-oriented financial institution, to contribute to and set up a credit rating arm. The arm may also attract capital from other countries and different sectors and integrate more related resources to provide commercialized credit rating services for the BRI.

Second, China should value the importance of rating results application. An experiment of basing the pricing of capital and financial products on B&R credit ratings can be launched in the financial markets of B&R countries so as to sharpen the international influence of the credit rating agency and improve services for companies of B&R nations. A fresh, extensive and representative rating system which can objectively reflect credit rating levels of developing nations and emerging market economies by country, industry and enterprise can coexist with the top three international credit rating agencies (Standard & Poor's, Fitch and Moody's).

Third, the country should step up cooperation with Standard & Poor's, Fitch and Moody's. The credibility and influence of B&R ratings will be enhanced step by step by developing a whole set of rating indicators system on the basis of advanced international rating technologies and attracting outstanding rating professionals. Besides, the B&R credit rating agency and the three international credit rating agencies feature an equal and mutually beneficial cooperative relationship rather than a competitive relationship. The B&R credit rating agency must learn from the good experience of international rating agencies and continuously strengthen core competitiveness.

11.2.3. *Continuing to strengthen legal services*

First, based on big data technology, China should comprehensively sort out the laws and regulations of countries involved in the BRI, integrate them into a dynamically updated database and address the difficulty in inquiring about laws and regulations and thereby comprehend the specific legal provisions as well as possible. Besides, an industry association of law firms in B&R countries should be established to be responsible for the development, maintenance and daily operation of the database. In addition, an official platform for exchanges and cooperation of practicing lawyers in B&R countries should be put in place to minimize the legal service barriers caused by asymmetry of legal systems and legal information.

Second, lowering the entry barrier to each B&R country's legal service industry is a yet to be resolved thorny issue. Law firms should extend their service reach and provide better legal services for enterprises' investing and financing activities through both internationalization and localization. The Chinese government should support Chinese law firms specialized in the economic and financial fields to develop foreign-related legal services. In addition, law firms can play an important role in debt recovery and help companies recover losses according to local laws by fully capitalizing on the positive externalities of their professional services.

Third, high-caliber lawyers or teams of lawyers who are professional and have a good command of lesser-known languages should strengthen collaboration and cooperation, and provide premier legal services for projects under the BRI specific to investment and financing structures, national features and project characteristics. A team of lawyers from law firms of the host country and the target country may be set up for the initiative's significant projects, and it may provide efficient and effective services based on the actual situation of the project, the investment and financing structure and the legal characteristics of the target country.

Fourth, recognizing the huge differences in legal systems, B&R countries should exert their best efforts to sign legally effective bilateral/multilateral agreements, and resolve institutional issues law firms and other intermediary service agencies cannot address through intergovernmental negotiations, thus expanding the space of legal services.

11.2.4. *Improving information service quality and database*

First, an investment and financing information platform led by the government and involving market entities should be launched by integrating data resources from different levels so as to provide necessary information for enterprises' market expansion and risk management. Governments of countries involved in the BRI should encourage intermediary service providers such as consulting and advisory companies and strategic plan design companies to expand information provision and analysis business and create a multi-dimensional database with national features at the macro level, industrial characteristics at the meso level and corporate characteristics at the micro level.

Second, intermediary service providers should improve the quality of country risk information and establish a country risk data and indicator system closely associated with investment and financing that can fully mirror risk profiles of countries involved in the BRI. It is necessary to strengthen information mining and analysis because companies now do not need the basic information on country risks but deeply processed information on the basis of long-term dynamic tracking and national database.

Third, intermediary service providers should build a special industry risk research and service system, provide overriding consideration to industrial information at the meso level, strengthen investigations of industries prioritized by countries involved in the BRI, largely demanded by the market or encouraged by host nations to attract foreign capital, and develop reliable information collection methods and industrial information access channels. This should be accompanied by the integration of relevant information on the country-industry dimension and focus of services on gathering and analyzing information of key countries and key industries.

Last, at the level of buyers' risk information, intermediary service providers should gain increasingly wider access to information on buyers in general trade and ensure the authenticity of such information, and continue to broaden information access channels in high-risk countries. They should also offer special information services for big players, prepare special information reports on big buyers and big companies based on the first-hand information gained from local information channels and provide overall information on counterparties for investors and financiers to draw references.

11.3. Reinforcing cross-border tax and anti-avoidance management

Tax policy is one of the key factors in deciding whether to conduct overseas investment and financing. It can directly affect companies' operating costs and economic performance, or even the success of the entire project. How to build an effective investment-related tax structure and forestall potential tax risks is particularly important to companies expanding business in foreign markets.

Enterprises which carry out engineering contracting, investment and other business activities abroad need to handle complicated taxes, including sales tax, import linkage tax, export linkage tax, value added tax, stamp duty, dividend or dividend withholding tax, interest withholding tax, capital gains tax, corporate income tax and personal income tax. These taxes can be simply divided into four categories: turnover taxes, income taxes, property taxes and miscellaneous taxes. Turnover taxes mainly consist of business tax, consumption tax, value added tax, import duty, export duty, license tax, stamp duty and resource tax; income taxes are mainly made up of corporate income tax, personal income tax, interest or dividend withholding tax and capital gains tax; property taxes primarily include fixed asset tax, real estate tax and land tax; miscellaneous taxes refer to all the other taxes that may be collected by national or local governments under all kinds of names (e.g., highway construction maintenance tax, educational surcharge tax, infrastructure construction tax and environmental protection tax).

In developing foreign business, enterprises should pay taxes to Chinese tax authorities in accordance with China's tax laws, and handle tax registration, declaration and payment in compliance with regulations. They should also pay taxes to the tax authorities of host countries based on their operating and investing activities there. Bilateral or multinational tax treaties are required to address the differences or conflicts of interest in tax systems or tax rates in different countries.

As of June 2018, China has signed double taxation avoidance agreements with 106 countries and regions, reducing double taxation on multinationals, easing companies' tax burdens, effectively safeguarding the legitimate rights and interests of multinationals and creating a good investment environment for going-global companies. Specifically, China has entered into bilateral tax treaties with 53 countries involved in the

BRI. And the tax treaties with Russia, Singapore, Estonia, Latvia, Uzbekistan and Romania have been fully or partially revised. In the next step, China will actively negotiate with the B&R countries with which it has not signed tax treaties, especially those having capacity cooperation with China.

If an investor has a tax dispute with the tax authority of the host country or believes it has been unfairly treated when enjoying tax treatment under the applicable tax treaty, it should request the Chinese tax authority to negotiate with the counterpart in the host country as per the "Mutual Agreement Procedure" under the tax treaty. Mutual Agreement Procedure (MAP) is a dispute resolution facility provided under the international avoidance of double taxation agreements, through which contracting states resolve tax-related issues. Under MAP, two countries negotiate on how to interpret specific terms of the treaty, resolve new issues arising from the actual implementation process and settle disputes between an enterprise of one country and the tax authority of another. In order to ensure the effective implementation of the treaty, both the OECD Model Tax Convention and the United Nations Model Double Taxation Convention contain provisions on MAP in the "Special Provisions" section.

The Chinese tax authority has done a lot of work in strengthening mutual agreement with the tax authorities of contracting states, resolved many tax disputes and unfair treatments encountered by Chinese enterprises abroad and helped Chinese companies properly handle a number of influential overseas tax cases. The State Administration of Taxation has opened a special channel for accepting tax disputes based on MAP to recover tax losses for cross-border taxpayers. So far, the Chinese tax authority has negotiated with relevant countries on more than 190 tax cases, and reduced nearly 30 billion yuan of international double taxation for multinationals.

Most companies choose to invest in target countries or regions via an intermediate holding company which enjoys a low tax rate for purposes such as relaxing overall tax burdens (i.e., tax planning with the aim of leveraging a more optimized tax treaty network, etc.), keeping information confidential, facilitating financing or IPO, more conveniently managing the investments in different countries or regions, and extending global reach in the future.

First, these kinds of companies should thoroughly understand or study the Chinese and foreign tax systems and regulatory environments related to the intermediate investment structure, including the potential effects of investment destination, the location of the intermediate holding company to be selected and China's relevant tax laws on the investment structure and future operation. The second consideration should be given to whether the intermediate holding company established in an area with a low tax burden has "reasonable business purposes" or "substantial business activities", or whether there is sufficient evidence to prove the existence of such "reasonable business purposes" or "substantial business activities". For the intermediate holding company, the existence of "substantial business activities" is not only a prerequisite for enjoying certain types of preferential treatment under the tax treaty between China and the invested country but can also effectively ensure it will not fall under tax controls over controlled foreign companies set forth in the income tax law. Third, the results of related party transactions should avoid triggering transfer pricing and anti-tax avoidance rules in relevant countries or regions, e.g., the invested country or the one where the intermediate holding company is located. This requires enterprises to have a deep understanding of the tax rules on transfer pricing in the relevant countries to prevent transfer pricing investigations and adjustments. The core of anti-avoidance adjustments of transfer pricing is to match enterprise functions with the analysis. Tax arrangements that do not have a reasonable business purpose, or transaction arrangements of related party transactions that lead to mismatch between business results of different companies and their functions and risks, will be easily challenged by tax authorities. By reasonably setting and allocating functions and risks between different enterprises in a group, the group can reduce the transfer pricing adjustment risk to a certain extent.

11.4. Buttressing the alignment of industrial technical standards

Many countries in the world are unable to develop standards themselves. Voluntarily or under the guidance of assistance programs provided by advanced nations, they usually adopt the standards of the developed world like the United States and Europe. Take the United States as an example. Over the past decades, technical standards set by the country have been globally applied so that American companies have a huge influence and right of speech in relevant areas, and dominate goods sales and service provisions in overseas markets, benefitting the economy a lot. These standards have, in a way, underpinned the global hegemony of the United States.

Chinese companies have accumulated a wealth of experience and capabilities in the construction of a series of large and complex projects in the mainland. This puts them in a superior position to support infrastructure construction under the BRI. However, due to historical reasons, China's technical standards of engineering are very different from those of developed countries, e.g., the standards of the United States, the United Kingdom, and Europe, and have been in an "isolated" state for a long time, although China's technical level is not necessarily low. This, coupled with the confinement of the country's engineering consulting services within borders, has hampered the worldwide recognition of Chinese standards, and they are seldom applied to international engineering projects. Consequently, the export of China's equipment and materials is restricted, and Chinese enterprises have to bear heavier construction costs due to unfamiliarity with international standards.

China, in advancing the BRI, should pay more attention to the alignment of industrial technical standards and enable the standards to play a fundamental and supportive role. In view of the fact that Chinese standards have not been widely recognized in the world and are seldom applied in international engineering projects, China should set up a management body of technical standard "internationalization" for organizing and coordinating relevant government departments, professional organizations and companies to pursue standard internationalization together. Chinese consulting service agencies should adapt themselves better to the global market, continuously improve competitiveness, carry out more research on internationalization strategies and basic topics, and provide a stronger boost to the going-global drive of Chinese standards. China should pilot the improvement of a complete set of standard systems with reference to general international standards in the areas where the country's technical standards are leading, and strive to introduce such standards to the whole world at the same time as launching projects all over the globe, in a bid to set an example for the successful application of Chinese engineering standards and demonstrate them fully. The government should issue relevant policies, giving projects that adopt Chinese standards preferential treatments on financing rate, insurance premiums and tax in line with the practices of international financial institutions. Professional associations should be encouraged to actively contact relevant international industry organizations, especially those in countries involved in the BRI or other related nations, and build a communication and exchange mechanism to promote the internationalization of Chinese standards.

Bibliography

Bai Yunzhen. The Belt and Road Initiative and the Transformation of China's Foreign Aid. *World Economics and Politics*, 2015, 11: 53–71,157–158.

Chen Jie et al. Importance of China–Pakistan Anti-Money Laundering Financial Intelligence Agency Cooperation to the Belt and Road Initiative. *Northern Finance*, 2017, 9: 10–14.

Chen Suwen. Some Thoughts on Strengthening International Tax Management. *Review of Economic Research*, 2015, 41: 6–8.

Cheng Leonard K.Three Questions on China's "Belt and Road Initiative". *China Economic Review*, 2016, 40: 309–313.

China Bond Rating Co., Ltd. and Institute of World Economy and Politics, Chinese Academy of Social Sciences, *China's Foreign Direct Investment and Country Risk Report (2017)*, Beijing: Social Sciences Academic Press, 2018.

China Center for Contemporary World Study. *Report on Strengthened People-to-People Ties under the Belt and Road Initiative*. Beijing: People's Publishing House, 2018.

Ding Fang and Lin Xiaoyan. Research on China's Labor Export under the Belt and Road Initiative. *Journal of Jinling University of Science and Technology*, 2016, 30(1): 53–56.

Feng Chong et al. Research on the International Labor Issues of the Belt and Road Initiative. *Legality Vision*, 2016, 29: 36–71

Gang Tianshi. New Expansion of China's International Cooperation Against Corruption. *Social Sciences Abroad*, 2017, 6: 150–152.

Gao Yan, Yang Tong, Zheng Gantian, Long Ziwu and Du Weigong. Research on the Status Quo and Influence Factors of Significant Shareholders' Reduction in Full Circulation. *Macroeconomic Research*, 2016, 8: 107–115.

Guan Fu. Analysis of Compliance Risks in Enterprises' Going Global Initiative. *International Project Contracting and Labor Services*, 2018, 4: 24–26.

Guo Ruixuan. In-Depth Participation in Global Cooperation to Improve Tax Governance. *China Taxation News* (A01), November 10, 2015.

Hua Yong. Legal Protection of Overseas Labor Rights under the Belt and Road Initiative. *Jianghuai Tribune*, 2016, 4: 114–119.

Huang Y. Understanding China's Belt & Road Initiative: Motivation, Framework and Assessment. *China Economic Review*, 2016, 40: 314–321.

Jiang Yuechun. *The Impact of China's Belt and Road Initiative on the World Economy*. Beijing: China International Studies Foundation, March 2016.

Jin J. *The True Intent behind China's AIIB Strategy*. Tokyo: Fujitsu Research Institute, 2015.

Li Jianjun and Li Juncheng. Belt and Road Infrastructure Construction, Economic Development and Financial Factors. *Studies of International Finance*, 2018, 2: 8–18.

Li Xiaoxi, Guan Chenghua and Lin Yongsheng. Positioning and Role of Environmental Protection in China's Belt and Road Initiative. *Environment and Sustainable Development*, 2016, 41(1): 7–13.

Liu Sisi. Belt and Road from the Perspective of the Theory of Difference Order Pattern: From European and American Thinking to Chinese Wisdom. *South Asian Studies*, 2018, 1: 1–14, 156.

Liu Yuechuan and Hu Wei. Foreign Anti-Corruption Law Enforcement Exposures to Chinese Enterprises and Responses. *Exploration and Free Views*, 2017, 8: 85–91.

Lu Guihua, Zhang Jing and Liu Baoliang. Voluntary Positive Performance Forecast of Chinese Listed Companies: For Public or Private Benefit – Empirical Evidence Based on Significant Shareholders' Reduction. *Nankai Management Review*, 2017, 20(2): 133–143.

Lu Jinyong, Wang Guang and Yan Shiqiang. Bilateral Investment Agreements and Protection of Investment Interests of Chinese Enterprises. *International Trade*, 2018, 3: 45–50.

Lu Wenchao. Research on the Prevention and Control of Corruption Risks in Overseas Investment of Enterprises under the Belt and Road Initiative. China Strategy, 2017.10 (Second Half). People's Tribune Frontiers, 2017, 20: 66–69.

Mei Guanqun. Research on India's Attitude toward the Belt and Road Initiative. *Asia Pacific Economics*, 2018, 2: 78–86.

Ming Hao. The Belt and Road Initiative and a Community with a Shared Future for Mankind. *Journal of Central University for Nationalities (Philosophy and Social Sciences)*, 2015, 6: 23–30.

Mo Pingfan. Research on the Belt and Road Initiative and Environmental Issues. *Business Information*, 2017, 18:25–27.

National Bureau of Statistics. *National Economic and Social Development Statistical Bulletin of the People's Republic of China*. Beijing: National Bureau of Statistics, 2017.

Nie Zilu, Liu Rupeng and Lian Jie. Anti-Corruption Law Urgently Needed in the Government Purchasing Sector for Promoting the Belt and Road Initiative. *Chinese Public Administration*, 2017, 12: 31–35.

Niu Yan and Wang Hua. Thoughts on Establishing China–Mongolia Anti-Money Laundering Cooperation Mechanism. *Northern Finance*, 2016, 9: 111.

Pan Yue and Chen Lusha. Labor Issues in Chinese Enterprises' Overseas Investment under the Belt and Road Initiative. *Around Southeast Asia*, 2018, 1: 84–90.

Pan Yue. Chinese Labor Issues in Indonesia under the Belt and Road Initiative. *Southeast Asian Studies*, 2017, 3:123–137, 157–158.

Qiu Bin, Zhou Qin, Liu Xiuyan and Chen Jian. A Summary of the Academic Symposium on "International Capacity Cooperation in the Context of the Belt and Road Initiative: Theoretical Innovation and Policy Research". *Economic Research*, 2016, 51(5): 188–192.

Rong Runsheng. *CSR and the "Going Global" Drive of Chinese Enterprises.* Hong Kong: Corporate Group of King & Wood, November 28, 2013. (www.chinalawinsight.com/2013/11/articles/corporate-ma/%E4%BC%81%E4%B8%9A%E7%A4%BE%E4%BC%9A%E8%B4%A3%E4%BB%BB%E5%92%8C%E4%B8%AD%E5%9B%BD%E4%BC%81%E4%B8%9A%E8%B5%B0%E5%87%BA%E5%8E%BB/)

Shao Mingchao. Corruption Prevention and Governance Countermeasures for Major Projects under the Belt and Road Initiative. *Macroeconomic Management*, 2017, 12: 37–40.

Song Shuang and Wang Yongzhong. Characteristics, Challenges and Countermeasures Concerning China's Financial Support for the Belt and Road Initiative. *International Economic Review*, 2018, 1: 108–123.

Sun Youhai. Research on Environmental Regulations of Green Belt and Road. *China Legal Science*, 2017, 6: 110–128.

Tang Yihong. Strengthening Economic and Trade Policy Coordination to Promote Economic and Trade Exchanges between China and B&R Countries. *Journal of International Trade*, 2018, 1: 9.

Tian Ze and Xu Dongmei. Efficiency of China's Investment in B&R Countries and Countermeasures. *Economic Survey*, 2016, 5: 84–89.

Wan Wei, Chen Kangxian and Chen Xiaomin. Research on China-ASEAN Free Trade Area Anti-Money Laundering Supervision Cooperation under the "Belt and Road" Framework. *Journal of Regional Financial Research*, 2015, 12: 50–53.

Wang Min, Chai Qingshan, Wang Yong, Liu Ruina, Zhou Qiaoyun, Jia Yuzhe and Zhang Lili. Implementation of the Belt and Road Initiative and International Financial Support Strategy. *International Trade*, 2015, 4: 35–44.

Wang Peizhi, Pan Xinyi and Zhang Shuyue. Institutional Factors, Bilateral Investment Agreements and Location Selection of China's Foreign Direct Investment: Based on Panel Data of Countries Involved in the Belt and Road Initiative. *Economic and Management Review*, 2018, 34(1): 5–17.

Wang Y. Offensive for Defensive: The Belt and Road Initiative and China's New Grand Strategy. *The Pacific Review*, 2016, 29(3): 455–463.

Wang Yidong. Current State, International Experience and Policy Recommendations in Respect of China's Outward Investment, Financing and Guarantees under the Belt and Road Initiative. *International Trade*, 2018, 2: 40–43, 52.

Wang Yiming. Innovating the Belt and Road Investment and Financing Mechanism for More Cooperation Opportunities. *China Economic Times*, June 19, 2017.

Wang Yiwei. How to Look at the Dispute over International Rules of the BRI?*FT Chinese Website*, February 22, 2018.

Wang Zhaoxing. *Creating a Financial Service Network to Pave the Way for the BRI.* Beijing, 2018. (http://finance.people.com.cn/n1/2018/0325/c1004-29887183.html)

Wu Wenhua and Fan Yijiang, Facility Connectivity of "Belt and Road Initiatives" has Achieved Fruitful Results. *China Reform Daily*. May 5, 2017. (www.cfgw.net.cn/2017-05/15/content_24509400.htm)

Wu Zhi and Zhong Yunyi. Research on the "General Exceptions" Clauses in China-Foreign Bilateral Investment Agreements. *Journal of Central South University*, 2017, 23(4): 18–26.

Xie Deren, Cui Chenyu and Liao Ke. Large Stock Dividends and Insiders' Shares Selling: Which One Dominates the Other? *Journal of Financial Research*, 2016, 11: 158–173.

Xu Deyou. The Belt and Road Initiative and Chinese Discourse in Global Governance. *Journal of Shantou University (Humanities and Social Sciences)*. 2018, 34(1):5–9, 94.

Xu Qiyuan, Yang Panpan and Xiao Lisheng. Building of Investment and Financing Mechanism for the Belt and Road Initiative: How China Can Participate More Effectively. *International Economic Review*, 2017, 5: 134–148.

Yang Siling. Governance and Challenges of the Relationship between China and Other B&R Countries under the Belt and Road Initiative. *South Asian Studies*, 2015, 2: 15–34, 154–155.

Ye Qi. Environmental Conflicts and Problems under the Belt and Road Initiative. *Modern Economic Research*, 2015, 5: 30–34.

Yu Jinping and Gu Wei. The Benefits, Risks and Strategies of the Belt and Road Initiative. *Journal of Nankai University (Philosophy and Social Sciences)*, 2016, 1: 65–70.

Yuan Jia. Exploring the Infrastructure Funding Demand and Investment and Financing Modes under the Belt and Road Initiative. *International Trade*, 2016, 5: 52–56.

Zhang Benbo. Policy Coordination among B&R Countries to Complement Each Other's Advantages and Benefit the Whole World. *Social Development Institute of the Chinese Academy of Macroeconomic Research*, May 15, 2017. (http://theory.gmw.cn/2017-05/15/content_24481065.htm)

Zhang Liping. Belt and Road Infrastructure Investment and Financing Needs and Promotion. *China Economic Times*, April 18, 2017.

Zhang Monan. Actively Building the Investment and Financing Framework and Cooperation System under the Belt and Road Initiative. *Securities Times*, July 19, 2016.

Zhang Peiyu. Promoting Connectivity of Policies and Standards for Improved Wide Consultation, Joint Contribution and Shared Benefits. *China Standardization*, 2017, 6:23–26.

Zhang Shuibo. Looking Internationally and Accelerated Alignment of Chinese Standards. March 18, 2018. (http://news.gmw.cn/2018-03/18/content_28018824.htm)

Zhang Yabin. Investment Facilitation under the Belt and Road Initiative and China's Foreign Direct Investment Choices: An Empirical Study Based on Multinational Panel Data and Investment Gravity Models. *Journal of International Trade*, 2016, 9: 165–176.

Zhang Yadi. The Belt and Road Initiative and China's Overseas Labor Protection. *International Outlook*, 2016, 8(3): 90–106, 146–147.

Zhang Yuan and Liu Li. Comparisons of Labor Markets in Countries along the Belt and Road and Aspirations. *World Economy and International Comparison*, 2017, 6:93–110.

Zhang Zhongyuan. *Building CSR-Related Soft Power of China's Going-Global Enterprises under the Belt and Road Initiative*. Beijing: Social Sciences Academic Press, April 2016.

Zhao Meng. Banks Lent over US$200 Billion to the BRI. *Financial Times*. April 27, 2018. (www.yidaiyilu.gov.cn/xwzx/gnxw/54181.htm)

Zhao Yan, Cui Yongmei and Zhao Libin. IPO, M&A, Stock Manipulation and Significant Shareholders' Reduction. *Journal of South China Normal University (Social Sciences)*, 2016, 3: 133–139.

Zhong Shi. Opening up the Financial Artery of the Belt and Road Initiative. *Economics*, 2017, Z2: 30–32.

Zhou Xiaochuan. Building the Belt and Road Investment and Financing Cooperation System via Wide Consultation and Joint Contribution. *China Finance*, 2017, 9: 6–8.

Zhu Qing. How to Get Deeply Involved in International Cooperation on Taxation. *China Financial and Economic News*, December 29, 2015.

Zhuang Yan. Analysis of the Effects of China's Belt and Road Initiative on International Political and Economic Relations. *Cultural Geography (Commentary)*. 2016, 20: 118.

Index